WITH HEALING

IN

HIS WINGS

WITH HEALING
IN
HIS WINGS

Camille Fronk Olson and Thomas A. Wayment
Editors

Brigham Young University
Easter Conference

RELIGIOUS STUDIES CENTER
BRIGHAM YOUNG UNIVERSITY

DESERET
BOOK

Published by the Religious Studies Center, Brigham Young University, Provo, Utah, in cooperation with Deseret Book Company, Salt Lake City.

http://rsc.byu.edu

Printed in the United States of America by Sheridan Books, Inc.

DESERET BOOK is a registered trademark of Deseret Book Company.

Visit us at DeseretBook.com.

Cover design and interior layout by Art Morrill.

White Hen with Chickens by Anton Ignaz Hamilton. Image courtesy of Wikimedia.

ISBN 978-0-8425-2836-8

US Retail: $17.99

Library of Congress Cataloging-in-Publication Data

BYU Easter Conference (2012 : Brigham Young University), sponsoring body.
With Healing in His Wings / Camille Fronk Olson and Thomas A. Wayment, editors.
    pages cm
Includes bibliographical references and index.
ISBN 978-0-8425-2836-8 (hard cover : alk. paper)
1. Easter—Congresses. 2. Jesus Christ—Mormon interpretations. I. Olson, Camille Fronk, editor. II. Wayment, Thomas A., editor. III. Title.

BX8643.J4B97 2012
232—dc23   2013000779

CONTENTS

By likening himself to a mother hen, the Savior testifies that he will cover us symbolically with his wings to save us.

FOREWORD

Camille Fronk Olson and
Thomas A. Wayment

WHEN POTENTIAL DANGER nears, a mother hen instinctively lifts her wings to protect her chicks and offers immediate refuge to them. When she lowers those ample wings to enfold her little ones, she stoically faces the source of danger. In her defensive posture, she creates a refuge that potentially places her life at risk. Interestingly, at times, prophets have compared various aspects of the Savior's ministry to the mother hen, teaching that he has healing in his wings. The Savior likewise used that metaphor to describe his own power to offer refuge to his followers. By likening himself to a mother hen, the Savior testifies that he will cover us symbolically with his wings to save us if we, like the chicks, will come to him.

His wings, however, do more than protect. He has gathered us in the past and will continue to gather us in the present and future "as a hen gathereth her chickens under her wings, if [we] will repent and return unto [him] with full purpose of heart" (3 Nephi 10:6; see also vv. 4–5). All of God's children are invited to be gathered, "or come to the knowledge of . . . their Redeemer" (1 Nephi 10:14; see also 15:14–15), where they will receive the saving covenants and ordinances of the gospel. Nowhere is the expansive reach of his merciful power more evident than in events associated with his Passion and victory over the grave—events that form the foundation of our Easter celebration. After Jesus was crucified for the sins of the world and lay in a tomb for three days, he rose from the dead "with healing in his wings" (2 Nephi 25:13; see also Malachi 4:2; 3 Nephi 25:2).

Because of his infinite Atonement, the Savior's capacity to heal is likewise ever- and far-reaching. In scripture, healing is metaphorically associated with wings. This lyrical language spoken by the ancients connotes "the power of the Atonement to overcome sin and death and 'to comfort all that mourn' (Isa. 61:2) and 'wipe away tears from off all faces' (Isa. 25:8; Rev. 21:4)."[1] The Prophet Joseph Smith received revelation that wings on God's creations in the Revelation of John are a "representation of power, to move, to act, etc." (D&C 77:4; see also Revelation 4:6–11). Jesus Christ rose from the dead with power to heal all manner of pains, temptations, and ills, his figurative healing wings working through the power of the Atonement. President Howard W. Hunter taught: "Whatever Jesus lays his hands upon lives. If Jesus lays his hands upon a marriage, it lives. If he is

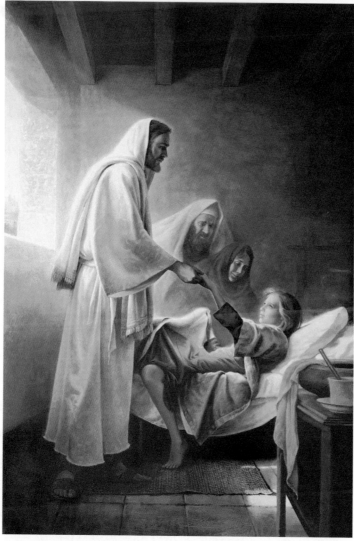

President Howard W. Hunter taught: "Whatever Jesus lays his hands upon lives. If Jesus lays his hands upon a marriage it lives. If he is allowed to lay his hands on the family, it lives." (Greg Olsen, *Christ Raising the Daughter of Jairus*, © Intellectual Reserve, Inc.)

allowed to lay his hands on the family, it lives."[2] There are no bounds to his capacity to succor or to limit those he can heal. As he encircles us with his almighty wings, he grants us power, confidence, and wisdom to invite others to come and renew hope for a better day.

Charles Wesley penned these stirring words, included in one of our hymns, to praise Jesus as the "lover of my soul":

Other refuge have I none;
Hangs my helpless soul on thee.
Leave, oh, leave me not alone;
Still support and comfort me.
All my trust on thee is stayed;
All my help from thee I bring.
Cover my defenseless head
With the shadow of thy wing.[3]

Every day of the year, but in a special way at Easter time, we reverence the supreme sacrifice that our God offered for us and rejoice in his magnanimous healing that he alone provides. The essays published in this volume were delivered at the annual Brigham Young University Easter Conferences in 2012 and 2013. May the presenters' insights, both academic and personal, enlighten your testimony of Jesus Christ and contribute to your celebration of the Easter season. Above all, we hope this collection will entice you to recognize and express gratitude for his healing power in your own life.

NOTES

1. David R. Seely, "Malachi Chapter Review: 3 Nephi 24–25 // Malachi 3–4," in *Book of Mormon Reference Companion*, ed. Dennis L. Largey (Salt Lake City: Deseret Book, 2003), 528.
2. Howard W. Hunter, "Reading the Scriptures," *Ensign*, November 1979, 64; see also Conference Report, October 1979, 93.
3. Charles Wesley, "Jesus, Lover of My Soul," *Hymns* (Salt Lake City: The Church of Jesus Christ of Latter-day Saints, 1985), no. 102.

The Resurrection is the crown jewel
of the plan of salvation.

RESURRECTION
"A MATTER OF
SURPASSING WONDER"

Elder Gary J. Coleman

IN DECEMBER 1961 a poster appeared on the walls of several campus buildings at Washington State University. It said that a young Mormon returned missionary was going to speak at the Student Union Building under the banner of the YMCA about "The Mormon Attitude of Life and Death." I contemplated whether or not I could go to the presentation. I was twenty years old and had been considering the ministry in the Catholic Church for the past decade of my life. An earnest wrestle for my soul began. Would I commit a mortal sin and enter the building that night to listen to the presentation about the Mormons? I entered that room and began

---

Elder Gary J. Coleman is an emeritus Seventy.

to learn the truth about the plan of salvation and the Resurrection. For the past fifty years, I have been on the journey to learn about the restored gospel of Jesus Christ. I will share the things of my soul.

Thousands of years ago the Lord spoke to Father Adam. In the sixth chapter of Moses, we read, "This is the plan of salvation unto all men, through the blood of mine Only Begotten, who shall come in the meridian of time. . . . All things have their likeness, and all things are created and made to bear record of me, both things which are temporal, and things which are spiritual; things which are in the heavens above, and things which are on the earth, and things which are in the earth, and things which are under the earth, both above and beneath: all things bear record of me" (Moses 6:62–63). Everything around us this Easter season supports this message: the birds are building their nests, the cows are having their calves, the sheep are having their lambs, the horses are having their foals, the flowers are blooming, and the trees are in full blossom. All things bear record of Him this Easter season.

The Bible that I had when I was a young man did not contain a topical guide, a dictionary, an index, or any pictures. However, in the Bible Dictionary accompanying the scriptures of The Church of Jesus Christ of Latter-day Saints we find this definition of the word *resurrection*: "The resurrection consists in the uniting of a spirit body with a body of flesh and bones, never again to be divided" (Bible Dictionary, "Resurrection," 761). On this and surrounding pages are other significant words such as *redemption, regeneration, repentance, replenish, restoration, restitution,* and *revelation.* All of those concepts make such a difference in the restored gospel of Jesus Christ, but today I will speak about the Resurrection, "a matter of surpassing wonder."[1]

BIBLICAL TEACHINGS

The word *resurrection* does not occur in the Old Testament, though there are many words like it. In the New Testament, however, the word *resurrection* occurs many times. In John 5, Jesus said, "For as the Father hath life in himself; so hath he given to the Son to have life in himself. . . . All that are in the graves shall hear his voice, and shall come forth; they that have done good, unto the resurrection of life; and they that have done evil, unto the resurrection of damnation" (John 5:26, 28–29). We learn here that all will be resurrected. From Luke we read, "Thou shalt be recompensed at the resurrection of the just" (Luke 14:14). And in John 11, we read these words from Jesus: "I am the resurrection, and the life: he that believeth in me, though he were dead, yet shall he live" (John 11:25).

The four Gospels, however, do not use the word *resurrection* surrounding the very event of Christ's Resurrection. Picture in your mind these various accounts: "He is not here: for he is risen" (Matthew 28:6). "He is risen; he is not here" (Mark 16:6). "He is not here, but is risen" (Luke 24:6). And then when the resurrected Christ meets with His disciples, we read, "Jesus himself stood in the midst of them, and saith unto them, . . . It is I myself: handle me, and see" (Luke 24:36, 39). "Jesus saith unto her, Mary. She turned herself, and saith unto him, . . . Master. Jesus saith unto her, Touch me not; for I am not yet ascended to my Father" (John 20:16, 17). And from 3 Nephi 11, "Behold my Beloved Son . . . hear ye him. . . . He came down and stood in the midst of them" (3 Nephi 11:7, 8). "Arise and come forth unto me, . . . feel the prints of the nails in my hands and in my feet" (3 Nephi 11:14).

In Acts 7, Stephen, full of the Holy Ghost, sees God and Jesus. He says, "I see . . . the Son of man standing on the right hand of God" (Acts 7:56). That would be the resurrected Jesus. In Acts 9, we read about Paul's conversion. A light shone around him, and a voice said, "Saul, Saul, why persecutest thou me? . . . I am Jesus whom thou persecutest" (Acts 9:4–5). And later, in Acts 26, Paul testifies, "I heard a voice speaking unto me. . . . And he said, I am Jesus. . . . I have appeared unto thee" (Acts 26:14–16). Again, the resurrected Jesus was seen. Other references in Acts through Revelation testify that many bore witness to the Resurrection of the Lord Jesus, the Resurrection of the dead, and the First Resurrection.

In your mind, are you seeing Christ through the eyes of those who saw Him? That is what scripture, vision, and latter-day prophecy have done for us. We can see Him through the eyes of others.

THE BOOK OF MOSES

There are so many places in the latter-day revelations where we learn of resurrection. Latter-day scripture is truly, for me, the treasure trove of information about the Resurrection. Early in this revelatory history, we have what is perhaps the first divine proclamation about the Resurrection: "This is my work and my glory—to bring to pass the immortality and eternal life of man" (Moses 1:39).

In Moses 6 the prophet Enoch speaks of the days of Christ thousands of years before His coming: "Jesus Christ [is] the only name which shall be given under heaven, whereby salvation shall come unto the children of men" (Moses 6:52). In verse 57, we read about the kingdom of God, in which the "Man of Holiness" dwells, "and the name of his Only Begotten is the Son of Man, even Jesus Christ" (Moses 6:57). Continuing, we read, "Enjoy the words of eternal life in this world, and eternal life in the world to come, even immortal glory" (Moses 6:59). Here we find many concepts associated with Resurrection: eternal life, salvation, glory, and kingdoms. What a wondrous thing to ponder on during Easter and springtime, when all things seem to come anew again and are symbolic of the Resurrection of Jesus Christ.

In Moses 7 we read a vision of things that were to come: "the saints arose" (v. 56), "the spirits . . . came forth" (v. 57), and "the Son of Man ascend[ed]" (v. 59). In addition, God says, "Truth will I send forth out of the earth, to bear testimony of mine Only Begotten; his resurrection from the dead; yea, and also the resurrection of all men" (v. 62). From the very beginning of mankind, God has taught His children that Christ would do a great work for all.

THE BOOK OF MORMON

The Book of Mormon prophets speak of the Resurrection of Christ hundreds of years before His divine birth. For example, in 1 Nephi 11, Nephi has a vision of Christ's life and ministry. In 1 Nephi 12, he has the vision of the Redeemer's life and ministry among the multitudes in the Americas.

The prophet Lehi says, "Redemption cometh in and through the Holy Messiah" (2 Nephi 2:6). This scripture introduces a new word to the text of the Book of Mormon: *redemption*. Afterward, Lehi says, "How great the importance to make these things known unto the inhabitants of the earth . . . that there is no flesh that can dwell in the presence of God, save it be through the merits, and mercy, and grace of the Holy Messiah, who layeth down his life according to the flesh, and taketh it again by the power of the Spirit, that he may bring to pass the resurrection of the dead, being the first that should rise" (v. 8). We must now ask ourselves, how are these truths made known? The answer is that we can know them through latter-day revelation and scripture.

In addition to teaching about the Resurrection, Book of Mormon prophets taught how the plan of God is in direct contrast to the plan of the evil one since the beginning. In 2 Nephi 9, Jacob writes of the great power of the Resurrection through the Redeemer. And yet in the same chapter we hear of the plan of the evil one because throughout our mortal time there is always going to be an effort that will be opposed to this work and this knowledge. To fulfill the merciful plan of the Great Creator, there needs to be a power of the Resurrection that will restore the bodies and spirits of men one to another. "O how great the plan of our God!" (2 Nephi 9:13). Before I became a convert to this Church, I had never heard the words "the plan of our God," "the plan of redemption," "the plan of mercy," or "the plan of restoration"! The grand idea of God's plan comes from latter-day revelation.

The Holy One of Israel wrought the Atonement for all who belong to the family of Adam so that the Resurrection might come to pass for all men, so that all might stand before Him at the great Judgment Day. The plan of Resurrection will come to pass with the sons and the daughters we have lost, the brothers and sisters, the mothers and fathers, the grandparents, the cousins, the friends and neighbors and prophets. Because of the Resurrection, they will live again!

The prophets Adam, Abinadi, Aaron, Samuel, and Moroni and the resurrected Lord Himself all speak of multiple facets of the Resurrection. Alma, like Paul, speaks of the different states of the soul between death and resurrection. Moroni, the concluding writer of the Book of Mormon, quotes the words of his father: "Ye shall have hope through the atonement of Christ and the power of his resurrection, to be raised unto life eternal, and this because of your faith in him" (Moroni 7:41). This seems to be a summary of the plan of salvation.

THE DOCTRINE AND COVENANTS

The Doctrine and Covenants mentions the Resurrection many times with wonderful illumination of the glorious doctrine in the Father's plan for us. Among the latter-day scriptures that discuss the Resurrection are sections 42, 45, and 63, which date from the early days of the Church, and then section 76, in which we see the contrast between the plan of God and the plan of the evil one once again. This vision from February 1832 is introduced by its two witnesses, Joseph Smith and Sidney Rigdon, who say, "Our eyes were opened and our understandings were enlightened, so as to see and understand the things of God" (D&C 76:12).

Let us see these things with them. They bear record of "the fulness of the gospel of Jesus Christ, . . . whom we saw and with whom we conversed in the heavenly vision" (v. 14). Continuing, they say, "We beheld the glory of the Son, on the right hand of the Father, . . . and saw the holy angels, and them who are sanctified. . . . He lives! For we saw him, even on the right hand of God" (vv. 20–23).

Now we see the opposite in the vision: "An angel of God who was in authority . . . who rebelled against the Only Begotten Son whom the Father loved . . . was thrust down from the presence of God" (v. 25). "Lucifer, a son of the morning" (v. 26), makes "war with the saints" (v. 29). He chooses to have people suffer, to "deny the truth and defy [God's] power" (v. 31). Section 76 also describes the sons of perdition as "vessels of wrath" (v. 33) and "the only ones who shall not be redeemed" (v. 38); Jesus "saves all except them" (v. 44).

In addition, we read from section 110, "We saw the Lord. . . . And his voice was as the sound of the rushing of great waters, even the voice of Jehovah, saying: . . . I am he who liveth" (D&C 110:2–4). Section 128 is also a glorious doctrinal presentation: "Herein is glory and honor, and immortality and eternal life—the ordinance of baptism by water, . . . to be immersed in the water and come forth out of the water is in the likeness of the resurrection of the dead" (D&C 128:12). Quietly, sacredly, by power and authority, baptism is repeated over and over again "in the likeness of the resurrection of the dead" (v. 12).

Sections 88, 130, 132, and 133 also speak of the Resurrection. Later we will speak more about the vision of the Father and the Son in section 137. Section 138 describes our Lord's visit to the spirit world, to those firm in the hope of a glorious resurrection.

THE PLAN OF SALVATION

So what is the key to the doctrine of the Resurrection? It is a correct knowledge of the Godhead. What is our first article of faith? "We believe in God, the Eternal Father, and in His Son, Jesus Christ, and in the Holy Ghost." What was the doctrine of God from the beginning? Elder Quentin L. Cook wrote,

Elder Quentin L. Cook
(© Intellectual Reserve, Inc.)

"Among the first principles lost in the Apostasy was an understanding of God the Father. It is not surprising, then, that among the first principles revealed in the Restoration was an understanding of God the Father. . . . Eternal life is to know the Father and His holy Son, Jesus Christ. Family relationships . . . extend beyond the grave. We can return to the presence of God, eternally united with our families."[2]

I condemn not the teaching of my faithful, religious parents— taking us to Mass, taking us to Bible School and to catechism lessons, repeating the rosary tens of thousands of times during my youth as we knelt in our living room and prayed. Our family's motto was "A family that prays together stays together."

I condemn not the religious teachers and mentors of my youth and early young adult years—Sister Teresa, Sister Mary Veronica, and Father O'Neil, who taught me the Latin of the Mass and how to respond as an altar boy for the next twelve years. I condemn not Father O'Donnell, Father Verdorn, and Father Graff, who took me with them on religious retreats to visit St. Edward's Seminary, St. Andrew's Seminary, and Mount St. Michael's Seminary to try to persuade me to become a Catholic priest. I believe that they did the best they could with what they had.

In John 17 we read, "These words spake Jesus, and lifted up his eyes to heaven, and said, Father, the hour is come; glorify thy Son, that thy Son also may glorify thee: as thou hast given him power over all flesh, that he should give eternal life to as many as thou hast given him. And this is life eternal, that they might know thee the only true God, and Jesus Christ, whom thou hast sent" (John 17:1–3). This scripture tells me that if we don't understand the Godhead correctly, we don't understand the doctrine of man's potential correctly.

In my first experience with the teachings of The Church of Jesus Christ of Latter-day Saints, I was drawn to a simple illustration of the plan of God. This first understanding occurred the night I described earlier, at the YMCA program. I knew the fear of serious sin for attending another church, the fear of damnation for seeking truth—hoping for heaven after this life but fearing hell. Those were burdens that I bore as I walked back and forth outside of that auditorium, as the presentation had already begun. I struggled to enter the room, because it would be an assault on the doctrine I had in my heart at that time, a mortal sin if I went in and listened to this returned missionary. Finally, I went in the room and joined with the audience, where that returned missionary taught me the plan of salvation.

The presentation was so clear and simple! I had never heard or seen such things before! But I knew I was learning the truth about God's plan. This plan had in it such words as *pre-earth, mortality, resurrection, judgment,* and *glory.* Several months later, someone gave me a Book of Mormon. Eighty-seven of its verses were marked, with notes referring me onward in my reading. You can get through the Book of Mormon in about thirty minutes if you read only eighty-seven verses. These scriptures were among the first five verses I read: "O how great the plan of our God!" (2 Nephi 9:13) and "He suffereth this that the resurrection might pass upon all men" (v. 22).

So I began to learn that the Resurrection is the crown jewel of the plan. In fact, Joseph Smith taught, "The fundamental principles of our religion are the testimony of the Apostles and Prophets, concerning Jesus Christ, that He died, was buried, and rose again the third day, and ascended into heaven; and *all other things which pertain to our religion are only appendages to it.*"[3] I am a living witness of the power of the restoration of this doctrine and a believer in the magnificent doctrine of the Resurrection. I learned, as the Prophet Jacob has taught, that "it is impossible that man should find out all his ways. And no man knoweth of his ways save it be revealed unto him; wherefore, brethren, despise not the revelations of God" (Jacob 4:8).

A WRESTLE WITH GOD

While I was growing up, I was taught that the Trinity was incomprehensible, that there could be no more scripture after the New Testament, and even that prophets in our day were false. When I learned of the Prophet Joseph Smith, I went through a terrible struggle. This wrestle with truth may be common to many people who grow up being taught false doctrines before they are introduced to the restored gospel. But because I had the opportunity to break through this struggle and accept Joseph as a prophet, it was a great day in my life. I know that truths taught in the latter days are ratified by the Holy Ghost, who will enable us to throw off the shackles and the burdens of the false teachings of men. I am a witness of the truths being restored in the last days.

The prophet Nephi taught that in the last days there would be many churches (see 2 Nephi 28:3). They would be full of men's doctrines, apostasy, and false teachers (see v. 4). He even said many people would say that there was no hell and no devil and that we did not need any more scripture (see vv. 21, 27). Nephi glories in plainness and condemns apostate doctrine wherever found in the world (see 2 Nephi 25:4). He says we cannot err nor misunderstand his teachings with respect to Christ (see v. 28). The prophets Mormon and

What power from the unseen world tried to prevent
this fourteen-year-old boy from learning the truth about
the Godhead, the Resurrection, and revelation?
(Walter Rane, *The Desires of My Heart*,
© Intellectual Reserve, Inc.)

Moroni taught of the evils of baptizing little children (see Moroni 8:8–9), transfiguring the word of God (see Mormon 8:33), forgiving sins for money, polluting doctrines, perverting the ways of the Lord, mocking God in abominations, and teaching wickedness in the name of religion (see Moroni 8:23). The true doctrine of the Resurrection is taught clearly and beautifully in the Book of Mormon by all the prophets cited therein.

So what preceded the First Vision? What power from the unseen world tried to prevent this fourteen-year-old boy from learning the truth about the Godhead, the Resurrection, and revelation? How powerful is the influence of darkness and confusion on the mind? How powerful is this opposition to the honest investigator? What happened to Joseph in this year? He said the Spirit moved him: "Never did any passage of scripture come with more power to the heart of man than this did at this time to mine. It seemed to enter with great force into every feeling of my heart. I reflected on it again and again . . . for how to act I did not know, and unless I could get more wisdom than I then had, I would never know" (Joseph Smith—History 1:12).

Have you ever been there—having to choose between remaining in "darkness and confusion" or, as Joseph Smith said, asking of God (v. 13)? God gives us agency that we might choose to leave a religion and enter the Lord's Church. The Spirit is a loving guidance to those who choose to do these things. It enables us to be free, free from false traditions and uninspired doctrines that bind and lead the soul captive.

Joseph Smith said, "I *must* . . . ask of God" (v. 13; emphasis added). So Joseph acted on this determination. He continued, "I retired to the woods. . . . It was the first time in my life that I had made such an attempt" to pray vocally (v. 14). "I was seized upon by some power which entirely overcame me, and had such an astonishing influence over me as to bind my tongue. . . . Thick darkness gathered around me, and it seemed to me for a time as if I were doomed to sudden destruction" (v. 15). Remember that he was only a boy! "[I exerted] all my powers to call upon God to deliver me out of the power of this enemy [this diabolical coward, this wretched enemy of truth] which had seized upon me . . . not . . . an imaginary ruin, but . . . the power of some actual being from the unseen world, who had such marvelous power as I had never before felt in any being" (v. 16).

Then came the light and the glorious deliverance! How many unseen beings had combined against him? Why would they combine against a mere boy? Is truth so precious, so wondrous, so filled with power that it actually frees one from the chains that bind? Yes! I know the freedom of this process that Jesus taught. I know that truth will make you free (see John 8:32)!

The Prophet Joseph Smith said, "It is the doctrine of the devil to retard the human mind, and hinder our progress."[4] He also said that "whatever we may think of revelation, . . . without it we can neither know nor understand anything of God, or the devil. . . . Without a divine communication [we] must remain in ignorance."[5] Satan's power is real. The Lord does not often make known the devil's evil workings, but sometimes we can know of them through our own experience with the awful presence of evil. Satan may even try to persuade the servants of God to give up their work. Satan knows that "where there is no kingdom of God there is no salvation. . . . Where the oracles of God are not, there the kingdom of God is not"![6]

In the Sacred Grove, the resurrected Jesus said to Joseph that he "must join none of them [the current sects and churches], for they were all wrong" (Joseph Smith—History 1:19). Jesus said that "all their creeds were an abomination," that "those professors were all corrupt," that "they teach for doctrines the commandments of men, having a form of godliness, but they deny the power thereof." Those rituals I had grown up with—transubstantiation, the baptism of children, Mary as a co-redeemer—were not the divine truth as Jesus had taught it.

The Prophet was often asked, "Wherein do you differ from others in your religious views?" He said, "One of the grand fundamental principles of 'Mormonism' is to receive truth; let it come from whence it may."[7] Further the Prophet said, "God has revealed His Son from the heavens and the doctrine of the resurrection also. I cannot find words to express myself. I care not what the theories of man are. We have the testimony that God will raise us up and he has the power to do it!" I am grateful that the teachings of my youth were enhanced, strengthened, and corrected by the glorious truths of the restored gospel of Jesus Christ.

At my mother's funeral mass, the priest in her parish was not present; he was on vacation. A substitute priest was asked to perform the mass, but he was going to be gone also. So the substitute for the substitute presided at my mother's funeral mass. But there was an elder of Israel there, and I told this man that I would give the sermon that day. He said, "Well, that would be highly unusual."

I said, "It *will* be unusual. I will teach of her life and her destiny through the Resurrection." He granted me permission to preach the sermon at the mass.

I gave that sermon because *we* have the doctrine of the Resurrection, the doctrine of eternal life, and the doctrine of the plan of salvation. The Doctrine and Covenants, the Book of Mormon, and the New Testament all speak about these last days, when incorrect doctrines would abound. But Jesus overcame the human predicament. He has all power over mortality and immortality. He has all power over resurrection, over redemption, over salvation, and over exaltation.

THE GLORIOUS DOCTRINE OF THE RESURRECTION

Let's now look at the words of this beautiful latter-day hymn:

While of these emblems we partake
In Jesus' name and for his sake,
Let us remember and be sure
Our hearts and hands are clean and pure.

For us the blood of Christ was shed;
For us on Calvary's cross he bled,
And thus dispelled the awful gloom
That else were this creation's doom.

The law was broken; Jesus died
That justice might be satisfied,
That man might not remain a slave
Of death, of hell, or of the grave,

But rise triumphant from the tomb,
And in eternal splendor bloom,
Freed from the pow'r of death and pain,
With Christ, the Lord, to rule and reign.[8]

Perhaps we could add another verse:

How wondrous thine eternal plan,
To help us come to thee again

In the almost two hundred years since Joseph Smith saw two personages, God the Father and His Only Begotten Son, standing above him in the air, the vast majority of the people of this earth have not learned of this wondrous truth pertaining to the Godhead.
(Del Parson, *First Vision*, © 1988 Intellectual Reserve, Inc.)

And live with those we dearly love,
All worthy of thy home above.

My own father, beset for thirty years by mental illness, died a ghastly death in August of 1984. His lonely and shrinking world had been most difficult for him. I know I will see him again in the glorious kingdoms of the Resurrection. The plain and precious doctrines of the Resurrection, though dismissed by the philosophies and false teachings of the world, are manifest in this gospel. In the almost two hundred years since Joseph Smith saw two personages, God the Father and His Only Begotten Son, standing above him in the air, the vast majority of the people of this earth have not learned of this wondrous truth pertaining to the Godhead. "There are many yet on the earth among all sects, parties, and denominations" who just don't know where to find this truth (D&C 123:12). Joseph said that many years ago, and it's still true today. Surely truth seekers everywhere would welcome latter-day revelations with respect to the True and Living God and His Glorified and Resurrected Son who have spoken to prophets in our time. But no. Man is content to expound creeds that remain an abomination in the sight of God and "teach for doctrines the commandments of men, having a form of godliness, but . . . deny the power thereof" (Joseph Smith—History 1:19).

While serving as a mission president, I was invited to a prayer breakfast in West Covina, California. I was accompanied by six

THE FAMILY

A PROCLAMATION TO THE WORLD

THE FIRST PRESIDENCY AND COUNCIL OF THE TWELVE APOSTLES
OF THE CHURCH OF JESUS CHRIST OF LATTER-DAY SAINTS

WE, THE FIRST PRESIDENCY and the Council of the Twelve Apostles of The Church of Jesus Christ of Latter-day Saints, solemnly proclaim that marriage between a man and a woman is ordained of God and that the family is central to the Creator's plan for the eternal destiny of His children.

ALL HUMAN BEINGS—male and female—are created in the to provide for their physical and spiritual needs, and to teach them to love and serve one another, observe the commandments of God, and be law-abiding citizens wherever they live. Husbands and wives—mothers and fathers—will be held accountable before God for the discharge of these obligations.

ordained of God. Marriage between man and [...]ntial to His eternal plan. Children are entitled [...] the bonds of matrimony, and to be reared by [...] mother who honor marital vows with com[...] Happiness in family life is most likely to be [...] founded upon the teachings of the Lord [...] successful marriages and families are estab[...] tained on principles of faith, prayer, repen[...]ness, respect, love, compassion, work, and [...]reational activities. By divine design, fathers [...] over their families in love and righteousness [...]nsible to provide the necessities of life and [...] their families. Mothers are primarily respon[...]nurture of their children. In these sacred re[...] fathers and mothers are obligated to help one [...]al partners. Disability, death, or other circum[...]necessitate individual adaptation. Extended [...]d lend support when needed.

[...]at individuals who violate covenants of [...] abuse spouse or offspring, or who fail to ful[...]ponsibilities will one day stand accountable [...] further, we warn that the disintegration of [...] ll bring upon individuals, communities, and [...] alamities foretold by ancient and modern [...]

[...]te responsible citizens and officers of gov[...]where to promote those measures designed [...]d strengthen the family as the fundamental [...]

[...]part of his message at the [...] Salt Lake City, Utah.

THE LIVING CHRIST

THE TESTIMONY OF THE APOSTLES
THE CHURCH OF JESUS CHRIST OF LATTER-DAY SAINTS

As we commemorate the birth of Jesus Christ two millennia ago, we offer our testimony of the reality of His matchless life and the infinite virtue of His great atoning sacrifice. None other has had so profound an influence upon all who have lived and will yet live upon the earth.

He was the Great Jehovah of the Old Testament, the Messiah of the New. Under the direction of His Father, He was the creator of the earth. "All things were made by him; and without him was not any thing made that was made" (John 1:3). Though sinless, He was baptized to fulfill all righteousness. He "went about doing good" (Acts 10:38), yet was despised for it. His gospel was a message of peace and goodwill. He entreated all to follow His example. He walked the roads of Palestine, healing the sick, causing the blind to see, and raising the dead. He taught the truths of eternity, the reality of our premortal existence, the purpose of our life on earth, and the potential for the sons and daughters of God in the life to come.

He instituted the sacrament as a reminder of His great atoning sacrifice. He was arrested and condemned on spurious charges, convicted to satisfy a mob, and sentenced to die on Calvary's cross. He gave His life to atone for the sins of all mankind. His was a great vicarious gift in behalf of all who would ever live upon the earth.

We solemnly testify that His life, which is central to all human history, neither began in Bethlehem nor concluded on Calvary. He was the Firstborn of the Father, the Only Begotten Son in the flesh, the Redeemer of the world.

He rose from the grave to "become the firstfruits of them that slept" (1 Corinthians 15:20). As Risen Lord, He visited among those He had loved in life. He also ministered among His "other sheep" (John 10:16) in ancient America. In the modern world, He and His Father appeared to the boy Joseph Smith, ushering in the long-promised "dispensation of the fulness of times" (Ephesians 1:10).

Of the Living Christ, the Prophet Joseph wrote: "His eyes were as a flame of fire; the hair of his head was white like the pure snow; his countenance shone above the brightness of the sun; and his voice was as the sound of the rushing of great waters, even the voice of Jehovah, saying:
"I am the first and the last; I am he who liveth, I am he who was slain; I am your advocate with the Father" (D&C 110:3–4).

Of Him the Prophet also declared: "And now, after the many testimonies which have been given of him, this is the testimony, last of all, which we give of him: That he lives!
"For we saw him, even on the right hand of God; and we heard the voice bearing record that he is the Only Begotten of the Father—
"That by him, and through him, and of him, the worlds are and were created, and the inhabitants thereof are begotten sons and daughters unto God" (D&C 76:22–24).

We declare in words of solemnity that His priesthood and His Church have been restored upon the earth—"built upon the foundation of . . . apostles and prophets, Jesus Christ himself being the chief corner stone" (Ephesians 2:20).

We testify that He will someday return to earth. "And the glory of the Lord shall be revealed, and all flesh shall see it together" (Isaiah 40:5). He will rule as King of Kings and reign as Lord of Lords, and every knee shall bend and every tongue shall speak in worship before Him. Each of us will stand to be judged of Him according to our works and the desires of our hearts.

We bear testimony, as His duly ordained Apostles—that Jesus is the Living Christ, the immortal Son of God. He is the great King Immanuel, who stands today on the right hand of His Father. He is the light, the life, and the hope of the world. His way is the path that leads to happiness in this life and eternal life in the world to come. God be thanked for the matchless gift of His divine Son.

THE FIRST PRESIDENCY   THE QUORUM OF THE TWELVE

January 1, 2000

Living apostles and prophets have often proclaimed the doctrine of the Resurrection.

men from other religions, and we were to speak of our belief in the Resurrection that Easter weekend. As these six religious men spoke, not one time was the Resurrection or Easter mentioned. It was left to the Mormon leader to speak of resurrection and eternal life through the Savior.

The Church of Jesus Christ of Latter-day Saints teaches about the doctrine of the Resurrection frequently. "The Family: A Proclamation to the World" speaks of these things. "The Living Christ" speaks of these things. In the Leadership Training Emphasis of the Church, we speak of preparing families for exaltation. From the *Encyclopedia of Mormonism*, we have this statement: "Resurrection is as universal as death. All must die and all must be resurrected. It is a free gift to all men. It is not the result of the exercise of faith or accumulated good works."[9]

From a 2008 special edition of the *Ensign* we read about the Lord Jesus Christ, and from a special edition of the *Ensign* in 2010 we read of the purpose of temples and the messages of the Resurrection and how we may help persons in our families who need the ordinances of salvation. In 2011, another special edition of the *Ensign* magazine featured the Book of Mormon and the plain and precious doctrines of the gospel of Jesus Christ. The first two lessons of *Preach My Gospel* teach of the Godhead and the Restoration, the plan of salvation, the Atonement, the Resurrection, the Final Judgment, immortality, and the kingdoms of glory. But very few people who receive those two lessons are eventually baptized. Along the way, the missionaries are turned aside, most likely because the teachings and philosophies of men have ensnared the lives of these investigators.

TEACHINGS OF CHURCH PRESIDENTS

In the past decade we have been learning in our Relief Society and priesthood meetings from eight volumes of the *Teachings of Presidents of the Church*. Following is a sample of lessons about the Resurrection from those manuals.

The Prophet Joseph Smith. "The heavens were opened upon us, and I beheld the celestial kingdom of God, and the glory thereof. . . . I also beheld that all children who die before they arrive at the years of accountability are saved in the celestial kingdom of heaven."[10]

"In knowledge there is power. God has more power than all other beings, because He has greater knowledge; and hence He knows how to subject all other beings to Him. He has power over all."[11]

Brigham Young. "Jesus is the first begotten from the dead, as you will understand. Neither Enoch, Elijah, Moses, nor any other man that ever lived on earth, no matter how strictly he lived, ever obtained a resurrection until after Jesus Christ's body was called from the tomb by the angel. He was the first begotten from the dead. He is the Master of the resurrection—the first flesh that lived here after receiving the glory of the resurrection. . . . Jesus had this power in and of himself; the Father bequeathed it to him; it was his legacy, and he had the power to lay down his life and take it again."[12]

John Taylor. "It now becomes our duty to enquire . . . what was accomplished by the atonement.

"First, the Resurrection. The penalty of the broken law in Adam's day was death; and death is passed upon all. The word of the Lord was, 'In the day that thou eatest thereof thou shalt surely die.' [Genesis 2:17; see also Moses 3:17.] The atonement made by Jesus Christ brought about the resurrection from the dead, and restored life. And hence Jesus said: 'I am the resurrection, and the life: he that believeth in me, though he were dead, yet shall he live;' (John 11:25) and Jesus Himself became the first fruits of those who slept."[13]

Wilford Woodruff. "The Savior Himself tasted of death; He died to redeem the world; His body was laid in the tomb, but it did not see corruption; and after three days it arose from the grave and put on immortality. He was the first fruit of the resurrection.

"I am satisfied, always have been, in regard to the resurrection. I rejoice in it. The way was opened unto us by the blood of the Son of God.

". . . This doctrine of the resurrection of the dead is most glorious."[14]

Heber J. Grant. "The perfect and absolute knowledge that we as Latter-day Saints have of the divinity of the work in which we are engaged, the absolute assurance that when life ends, if we have been faithful we are to have the pleasure and the privilege of going back into the presence of those whom we have loved and who have gone on before."[15] These doctrines can give us comfort through our trials in this life. My own dear convert sister and her faithful husband were baptized and confirmed by my brother and me and then sealed in the holy temple. They were killed in an automobile accident and left behind six orphans. But they had the ordinances necessary for eternal life, so their family can be reunited after death. They will be participants in the holy resurrection of the just.

George Albert Smith. "When Jesus was raised from the dead He became the first fruits of the resurrection. The spirit begotten of the Father (the intelligent part of His soul) reinhabited His earthly tabernacle which had been purified, and He became a glorified celestial being, and took His place, on the right hand of the Father, as one of the Godhead."[16]

"We accept without reservation the testimony of all the evangelists contained in the New Testament with reference to the resurrection of the Redeemer of mankind. It is so plain that it seems to me that no thoughtful person can fail to comprehend it."[17]

"In the day and age in which we live there arose another individual. . . . [Joseph Smith] not only had the witness of the Bible that Jesus was the Christ, but he saw God the Father standing in the clouds of heaven, clothed with glory, and Jesus Christ, the Redeemer of the world, exalted at His right hand, and he heard the voice of the Lord, saying, 'This is My Beloved Son, hear Him.' [See Joseph Smith—History 1:16–17.]"[18]

David O. McKay. "Establish it as a fact that Christ did take up His body and appeared as a glorified, resurrected Being, and you answer the question of the ages—'If a man dies, shall he live again?' [see Job 14:14.]

"That the literal resurrection from the grave was a reality to the disciples who knew Christ intimately is a certainty. . . .

"The latest and greatest confirmation that Jesus rose from the grave is the appearance of the Father and the Son to the Prophet Joseph Smith, nineteen hundred years after the event. . . . This miracle of life is significant not only in itself, but in its connotation of all the basic principles of true Christianity."[19]

Spencer W. Kimball. "Jesus of Nazareth was the one who, before the world was created, was chosen to come to earth to perform this service, to conquer mortal death. This voluntary action would atone for the fall of Adam and Eve and permit the spirit of man to recover his body, thereby reuniting body and spirit.

"This resurrection referred to is the work of Jesus Christ, the Savior, who, because he was both mortal (the son of Mary) and divine (the Son of God), was able to overcome the powers governing the flesh. He actually gave his life and literally took it up again as the 'first fruits,' to be followed by every soul that has ever lived [see 1 Corinthians 15:22–23]."[20]

President Thomas S. Monson often speaks of the Resurrection. For instance, he has said, "With all my heart and the fervency of my soul, I testify as a special witness that God does live. Jesus is his Son, the Only Begotten of the Father in the flesh. He is our Redeemer; he is our mediator with the Father. He it was who died on the cross to atone for our sins. He became the firstfruits of the resurrection. Oh, sweet the joy this sentence gives, 'I know that my Redeemer lives!'"[21] Resurrection was the theme of his general conference address in April 2012. In fact, during the April 2012 general conference, seven of our apostles and prophets spoke of the Resurrection, and the April 2012 issue of the *Ensign* had a Resurrection theme. We are not through learning and teaching about this doctrine!

CONCLUSION

I have spent the last two decades serving the Lord full-time, ten of those years in Latin America and the islands of the sea. I have seen the national cemeteries, the billboards, the highway memorials, the home shrines, and the tributes to the dead in newspapers and magazines. I have seen church buildings silent and decaying. I have seen the public mourning for the dead, and it is beyond comprehension, while private mourning is also beyond description. One thing prevails among the human family, and that is hope that someday they will see their family members and loved ones again. I testify that the restoration of the gospel of Jesus Christ has brought that hope to reality in the true doctrine of the Resurrection. Members of our Church have been participants in war and conflict among nations, but I am grateful that members of our Church have also been participants in the conflicts and wars for the minds and souls of men and have taught millions of Father's children the true gospel.

I know of the despair of living under the burdens of false doctrines and works of darkness that bind the mind and pervert the right ways of the Lord. I know the Lord has revealed greater knowledge of the Resurrection, one of the great and glorious doctrines of the gospel, reaffirmed in the restoration of eternal truths in these latter days. May I speak now for those of us who have found the gospel and all things pertaining to the kingdom of God and the His Beloved Son. I thank you, the missionaries and faithful members of the Church, for inviting us to leave the darkness and come into the light. Thank you for visiting with us, for praying for us, for sharing this precious gospel with us, and for teaching us truths that would change our lives that we may know for ourselves about God the Father and His precious Son through the Holy Ghost. I thank you for your fellowship, your friendship, and your discipleship, through which we, the converts of the Church, might come to know the truths of the gospel today. Your service to us has been marvelous. You have brought us hope in the Resurrection to eternal life through the things you have done for us. Thank you for teaching us who we really are as the people of the covenant in the house of Israel, to be numbered among those from the families of the earth to be blessed with this everlasting gospel of the Lord and Savior, Jesus Christ. I thank God that He has revealed these things to us in the last days.

NOTES

1. James E. Talmage, *The Articles of Faith* (Salt Lake City: Deseret Book, 1924), 77.
2. Quentin L. Cook, "The Doctrine of the Father," *Ensign*, February 2012, 33–34.
3. *Teachings of Presidents of the Church: Joseph Smith* (Salt Lake City: The Church of Jesus Christ of Latter-day Saints, 2007), 49; emphasis added.
4. *History of the Church of Jesus Christ of Latter-day Saints*, ed. B. H. Roberts, 2nd ed. rev. (Salt Lake City: Deseret Book, 1978), 5:24.
5. *Teachings of Presidents of the Church: Joseph Smith*, 387.
6. *History of the Church*, 5:257.
7. *History of the Church*, 5:499.
8. John Nicholson, "While of These Emblems We Partake," *Hymns* (Salt Lake City: The Church of Jesus Christ of Latter-day Saints, 1985), no. 174; I have added an additional verse to this hymn.
9. Douglas L. Callister, "Resurrection," in *Encyclopedia of Mormonism*, ed. Daniel H. Ludlow (New York: Macmillan, 1992), 3:1222–23.
10. *Teachings of Presidents of the Church: Joseph Smith*, 95.
11. *Teachings of Presidents of the Church: Joseph Smith*, 265.
12. *Teachings of Presidents of the Church: Brigham Young* (Salt Lake City: The Church of Jesus Christ of Latter-day Saints, 1997), 275.
13. *Teachings of Presidents of the Church: John Taylor* (Salt Lake City: The Church of Jesus Christ of Latter-day Saints, 2001), 50.
14. *Teachings of Presidents of the Church: Wilford Woodruff* (Salt Lake City: The Church of Jesus Christ of Latter-day Saints, 2004), 81.

15. *Teachings of Presidents of the Church: Heber J. Grant* (Salt Lake City: The Church of Jesus Christ of Latter-day Saints, 2002), 45.

16. *Teachings of Presidents of the Church: George Albert Smith* (Salt Lake City: The Church of Jesus Christ of Latter-day Saints, 2004), 74.

17. *Teachings of Presidents of the Church: George Albert Smith*, 24.

18. *Teachings of Presidents of the Church: George Albert Smith*, 26–27.

19. *Teachings of Presidents of the Church: David O. McKay* (Salt Lake City: The Church of Jesus Christ of Latter-day Saints, 2003), 65–66.

20. *Teachings of Presidents of the Church: Spencer W. Kimball* (Salt Lake City: The Church of Jesus Christ of Latter-day Saints, 2006), 27.

21. *Pathways to Perfection: Discourses of Thomas S. Monson* (Salt Lake City: Deseret Book, 1973), 8.

Our love for and observance of the Sabbath day or the Lord's day is forever changed and enhanced as we come to understand and remember that every Sunday, not only Easter Sunday, is the Lord's day.

EASTER, THE LORD'S DAY

Elder John M. Madsen

M Y UNDERSTANDING OF the meaning and significance of
Easter was forever changed in 1968 with the passing of our
infant son James Allen, our second-born child. Right after the funeral, my wife and I were riding in the hearse with that tiny white
casket before us and with loved ones and friends following behind.
Suddenly, we were overwhelmed with deep and inexpressible feelings of love for our son. I reached for the tiny casket and placed
it on my lap. I then released the simple hook and opened the lid,
and for a few precious moments we looked upon our son in loving
silence. I then reached in and took his tiny hand in mine and began

*Elder John M. Madsen is an emeritus General
Authority and a former associate professor of
ancient scripture at Brigham Young University.*

to express the deep feelings of my soul, saying, "James, you hadn't better sleep in on the morning of the Resurrection! Your mother and I will be looking for you, son!" And then, with all the love of our souls, I spoke of our determination to live the gospel of Jesus Christ in such a way as to be worthy of a glorious reunion with him on the morning of the Resurrection.

I, like each one of you, have had, and will have, many other experiences that will forever change and enhance and deepen our understanding of the meaning and supernal significance of Easter. Another such experience came for me during the Sunday morning session of general conference, held in the Tabernacle on Temple Square in April of 1996. President Gordon B. Hinckley was speaking, and he said:

> This is Easter morning. This is the Lord's day, when we celebrate the greatest victory of all time, the victory over death. Those who hated Jesus thought they had put an end to Him forever when the cruel spikes pierced His quivering flesh and the cross was raised on Calvary. But this was the Son of God, with whose power they did not reckon. Through His death came the Resurrection and the assurance of eternal life.

President Hinckley continued:

President Gordon B. Hinckley
(© Intellectual Reserve, Inc.)

> With sorrow unspeakable those who loved Him placed His wounded, lifeless body in the new tomb of Joseph of Arimathea. Gone was the hope from the lives of His Apostles, whom He had loved and taught. He to whom they had looked as Lord and Master had been crucified and His body laid in a sealed tomb. He had taught them of His eventual death and Resurrection, but they had not understood. Now they were forlorn and dejected. . . .
>
> The Jewish Sabbath passed. Then came a new day, a day that ever after was to be *the Lord's day*.[1]

Yet again, my understanding of the meaning and supernal significance of Easter was forever changed in April of the year 2000. I was listening to the video presentation by the First Presidency and Quorum of the Twelve Apostles entitled *Special Witnesses of Christ*. President Gordon B. Hinckley introduced this inspiring video presentation from a balcony of the Brigham Young University

Jerusalem Center for Near Eastern Studies, with the golden Dome
of the Rock on the Temple Mount and the city of Jerusalem as his
backdrop.

As part of his introduction, President Hinckley said, "Jerusalem
was the scene of the final days of the mortal life of the Son of God.
Here He suffered the agony of Gethsemane, His arrest, His trials,
His condemnation, the unspeakable pain of His death on the cross,
His burial in Joseph's tomb, and the triumphant coming forth in the
Resurrection." He continued:

> Now, 2,000 years have come and gone since His birth
> in Bethlehem. Surely this is a time for remembrance and
> recommitment. In our day the Lord has called 15 *special
> witnesses* to testify of His divinity before all the world.
> Theirs is a unique calling; they are Apostles of the Lord
> Jesus Christ, chosen and commissioned by Him. They
> have been commanded to bear witness of His living real-
> ity by the power and authority of the holy apostleship in
> them vested.[2]

President Hinckley explained that "these special witnesses" would
"speak . . . from various locations around the earth."[3] Then, after ten
of his Brethren had spoken, President Hinckley spoke, as a *special
witness*, standing in front of the Garden Tomb. He said:

Just outside the walls of Jerusalem, in this place or some-
where nearby, was the tomb of Joseph of Arimathea where
the body of the Lord was interred. On the third day following His burial "came Mary Magdalene and the other
Mary to see the sepulchre.

"And, behold, there was a great earthquake: for the
angel of the Lord descended from heaven, and came and
rolled back the stone from the door, and sat upon it. . . .

"And the angel . . . said unto the women, Fear not ye:
for I know that ye seek Jesus, which was crucified.

"He is not here: for he is risen, *as he said*.[4] Come, see
the place where the Lord lay" (Matt. 28:1–2, 5–6).

President Hinckley then said: "These are the most reassuring words
in all of human history. Death—universal and final—had now been
conquered. 'O death, where is thy sting? O grave, where is thy victory?' (1 Cor. 15:55). To Mary, the Risen Lord first appeared. He
spoke to her, and she replied. He was real. He was alive, He whose
body had been laid in death." President Hinckley then declared:
"Never had this occurred before. There had been only death without
hope. Now there was life eternal. Only a God could have done this.
The Resurrection of Jesus Christ was the great crowning event of His
life and mission. It was the capstone of the Atonement. The sacrifice
of His life for all mankind was not complete without His coming

forth from the grave, with the certainty of the Resurrection for all who have walked the earth."

President Hinckley continued:

> Of all the victories in the chronicles of humanity, none is so great, none so universal in its effects, none so everlasting in its consequences as the victory of the crucified Lord, who came forth from the tomb that first Easter morning. . . .
>
> All [those] who saw and heard and spoke with the Risen Lord, testified of the reality of this greatest of all miracles. His followers through the centuries lived and died in proclamation of the truth of this supernal act.
>
> To all of these we add our testimony that He who died on Calvary's cross arose again in wondrous splendor as the Son of God, the Master of life and death.[5]

Before continuing, I wish to briefly summarize President Hinckley's teachings regarding Easter:

- Easter is the Lord's day and "ever after was to be the Lord's day."[6]
- Easter is the celebration of the Resurrection of Jesus Christ, which "was the great crowning event of His life and mission. It was the capstone of the Atonement."[7]

- "Through His death came the Resurrection and the assurance of eternal life."[8]

- "The sacrifice of His life for all mankind was not complete without His coming forth from the grave, with the certainty of the Resurrection for all who have walked the earth."[9]

- "Of all the victories in the chronicles of humanity, none is so great, none so universal in its effects, none so everlasting in its consequences as the victory of the crucified Lord, who came forth from the tomb that first Easter morning."[10]

Regarding the Lord's day, or the Sabbath day, Elder Bruce R. McConkie of the Quorum of the Twelve Apostles taught:

Sabbath observance is an eternal principle, and the day itself is so ordained and arranged that it bears record of Christ by pointing particular attention to great works he has performed. From the day of Adam to the Exodus from Egypt, the Sabbath commemorated the fact that Christ rested from his creative labors on

Elder Bruce R. McConkie
(© Intellectual Reserve, Inc.)

the 7th day. (Ex. 20:8–11.) From the Exodus to the day of his resurrection, the Sabbath commemorated the deliverance of Israel from Egyptian bondage. (Deut. 5:12–15.) . . . From the days of the early apostles to the present, the Sabbath has been the first day of the week, the Lord's Day, in commemoration of the fact that Christ came forth from the grave on Sunday. (Acts 20:7.)[11]

Our love for and observance of the Sabbath day, or the Lord's day, is forever changed and enhanced as we come to understand and remember that every Sunday, not only Easter Sunday, is the Lord's day, "in commemoration of the fact that Christ came forth from the grave on Sunday."[12]

I wish to share one other experience that had a profound effect upon me and upon my understanding of the meaning and supernal significance of Easter. Many years ago while working at Church headquarters, I noticed an announcement that Elder McConkie would be speaking in a noon devotional in the First Floor Auditorium of the Church Office Building. Rather than going to lunch, I went directly to the auditorium, which quickly filled to capacity. Elder McConkie gave a powerful discourse on the consequences of the Fall, and as he concluded he asked this question, "How do you prove that Jesus is the Christ?" There was a profound silence. No one moved or offered any response. Then Elder McConkie declared, "It all centers in the

Resurrection." Elder McConkie then asked, "How do you prove the Resurrection?" Once again there was a profound silence until Elder McConkie finally declared, "It all centers in witnesses."

This was a glorious moment for me as there, standing before us, was an Apostle of the Lord Jesus Christ, a *special witness*. How do you prove that Jesus is the Christ? It all centers in the Resurrection. How do you prove the Resurrection? It all centers in witnesses.

Let's consider the first question, with some modification and additions. How did Jesus—the crucified Lord, who died on Calvary's cross, was buried in Joseph's tomb, and rose again the third day—prove to his Apostles and faithful disciples that He was indeed the Christ?

For an answer we turn to Luke 24, beginning with verse 33, wherein we read that the two disciples who had just beheld the Risen Lord "rose up the same hour, and returned" from the village of Emmaus "to Jerusalem, and found the . . . [Apostles] gathered together, and them that were with them." Surely these two disciples could scarcely contain their joy or be constrained from reporting the wondrous experience they had just had with the Risen Lord (see vv. 13–32). But first, they were greeted with the glorious announcement that "*the Lord is risen indeed, and hath appeared to Simon,*" the Lord's chief Apostle. And then the two disciples were permitted to tell "what things were done in the way, and how [Jesus] was known of them in breaking of bread" (vv. 33–35; emphasis added).

And as they thus spake, [now, try to imagine that you were present as] Jesus himself [suddenly appeared and] stood in the midst of them, and saith unto them, Peace be unto you.

But they were terrified and affrighted, and supposed that they had seen a spirit.

And he said unto them, Why are ye troubled? and why do thoughts arise in your hearts?

Behold my hands and my feet, that it is I myself: handle me, and see; for a spirit hath not flesh and bones, as ye see me have.

And when he had thus spoken, he shewed them his hands and his feet.

And while they yet believed not for joy, and wondered, he said unto them, Have ye here any meat?

And they gave him a piece of a broiled fish, and of an honey-comb.

And he took it, and did eat before them.

And he said unto them, These are the words which I spake unto you, while I was yet with you, that all things *must* be fulfilled, which were written in the law of Moses, and in the prophets, and in the psalms, concerning *me*. (Luke 24:36–44; emphasis added)

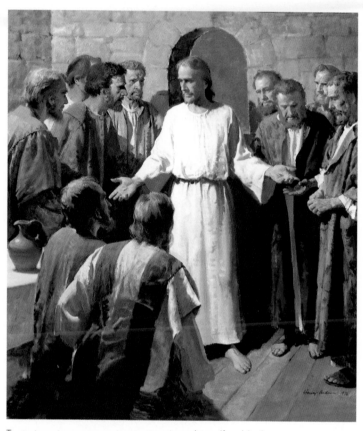

Try to imagine you were present as Jesus himself suddenly appeared and stood in the midst of the Apostles.
(Harry Anderson, *Feeling the Prints in His Hands*,
© Intellectual Reserve, Inc.)

He said this to the disciples, some of whom had been with him almost daily for about three years. "Then opened he their understanding, that they might understand the scriptures" (v. 45) as never before and that they might see and understand who it was that was standing before them and teaching them; that they might see and understand that all things that were written in the law of Moses, and in the prophets, and in the psalms concerning *Him* can be simply summarized in what *He, the Risen Lord Jesus Christ*, was about to say to them.

> And [He] said unto them, Thus it is written, and thus it behoved Christ [or thus it was necessary for Christ] to suffer, and to rise from the dead the third day:
>
> And that repentance and remission of sins should be preached in his [the Risen Lord's] name among all nations, beginning at Jerusalem.
>
> And ye are *witnesses* of these things. (vv. 46–48; emphasis added)

None present on that glorious and wondrous occasion could possibly misunderstand Jesus' own words and testimony, confirming that He Himself was indeed the Christ, or that He was indeed the long-awaited and promised Messiah.

And from John 20:24 we read that "Thomas, one of the twelve, . . . was not with them when Jesus came," on what Elder James E. Talmage calls "the evening of the Resurrection Sunday." Elder Talmage observes that Thomas remained "unconvinced," in spite of the "solemn testimony" of what his brethren and sisters "had seen, heard, and felt,"[13] exclaiming, "Except I shall see in his hands the

I can see in my mind's eye Thomas, humbly reaching his
hand toward the Savior's outstretched hands and doing
just as the Risen Lord had bidden him to do.
(Carl Bloch, *The Doubting Thomas*, 1881. Courtesy of the
Museum of National History at Frederiksborg Castle.)

print of the nails, and put my finger into the print of the nails, and thrust my hand into his side, I will not believe" (John 20:25). "A week later . . . on the next Sunday, which day of the week afterward came to be known to the Church as the 'Lord's Day,'"[14] the disciples again assembled, "and Thomas with them: then came Jesus, the doors being shut, and stood in the midst, and said, Peace be unto you. Then saith he to Thomas, Reach hither thy finger, and behold my hands; and reach hither thy hand, and thrust it into my side: and be not faithless, but believing" (John 20:26–27).

At that moment, I can see in my mind's eye Thomas, humbly reaching his hand toward the Savior's outstretched hands and doing just as the Risen Lord had bidden him to do—namely, putting his finger "into the print of the nails" and thrusting his "hand into his side." And then "Thomas answered and said unto him, My Lord and my God" (John 20:28). How do you prove that Jesus is the Christ? It all centers in the Resurrection. How do you prove the Resurrection? It all centers in witnesses.

Just eight days after the crucified Lord came forth from the tomb, many of His faithful disciples and all of His living Apostles had seen the Risen Lord and heard Him speak and had handled or felt His resurrected body. And in so doing, they had become *witnesses*.

In John 20:30–31 we read, "And in many other signs truly did Jesus in the presence of his disciples, which are not written in this book: but these are written that ye might believe that Jesus is the

Christ, the Son of God; and that believing ye might have life through his name."

And from the book of Acts 1:1–3 we read these words, written by Luke, "the beloved physician" (see Colossians 4:14):

> The former treatise have I made . . . of all that Jesus began both to do and teach,
>
> Until the day in which he was taken up, after that he through the Holy Ghost had given commandments unto the apostles whom he had chosen:
>
> To whom also he *shewed himself alive* after his passion [or sufferings; Joseph Smith Translation] by many infallible proofs, being seen of them forty days, and speaking of the things pertaining to the kingdom of God. (emphasis added)

How did Jesus, the Risen Lord, prove to the Nephites that He was indeed the Christ? "Jesus Christ did *show himself* unto the people of Nephi . . . and did minister unto them" (3 Nephi 11, heading; emphasis added). And when He appeared to them and confirmed to them His identity (see 3 Nephi 11:10–12), He bade them to come unto Him and thrust their hands into His side and "feel the prints of the nails in [His] hands and in [His] feet, . . . and this they did do, going forth one by one until they had all gone forth, and did

How did Jesus, the Risen Lord, prove to the Nephites that He was indeed the Christ? "Jesus Christ did show himself unto the people of Nephi . . . and did minister unto them" (3 Nephi 11, heading). (Simon Dewey, *Christ in America*, 2003, © Intellectual Reserve, Inc.)

see with their eyes and did feel with their hands and did know of a surety and did bear record, that it was he, of whom it was written by the prophets, that should come" (3 Nephi 11:14–15).

Speaking of the Resurrection of the Lord Jesus Christ, President Hinckley said:

> No event of history has been more certainly confirmed. There is the testimony of all who saw and felt and spoke with the risen Lord. He appeared on two continents in two hemispheres and taught the people. . . . Two sacred volumes, two testaments speak of this most glorious of all events in all of human history. . . .
>
> And then comes the ringing testimony of the Prophet of this dispensation that in a wondrous theophany he saw and was spoken to by the Almighty Father and the Risen Son. . . .
>
> There is nothing more universal than death, and nothing brighter with hope and faith than the assurance of immortality. The abject sorrow that comes with death, the bereavement that follows the passing of a loved one are mitigated only by the certainty of the Resurrection of the Son of God that first Easter morning.[15]

On Easter Sunday, April 4, 2010, our beloved living prophet, President Thomas S. Monson, spoke these comforting words:

President Thomas S. Monson
(© Intellectual Reserve, Inc.)

The empty tomb that first Easter morning was the answer to Job's question, "If a man die, shall he live again?" *To all within the sound of my voice, I declare, if a man die, he shall live again.* We know, for we have the light of revealed truth.

"For since by man came death, by man came also the resurrection of the dead.

"For as in Adam all die, even so in Christ shall all be made alive" (1 Corinthians 15:21–22).

President Monson continued:

I have read—and I believe—the testimonies of those who experienced the grief of Christ's crucifixion and the joy of His Resurrection. I have read—and I believe—the testimonies of those in the New World who were visited by the same risen Lord.

I believe the testimony of one who, in this dispensation, spoke with the Father and the Son in a grove now called sacred and who gave his life, sealing that testimony with his blood. Declared He:

"And now, after the many testimonies which have been given of him, this is the testimony, last of all, which we give of him: That he lives!"

To conclude his address, President Monson said:

My beloved brothers and sisters, in our hour of deepest sorrow, we can receive profound peace from the words of the angel that first Easter morning: "He is not here: for he is risen" (Matthew 28:6).

He is risen! He is risen!
Tell it out with joyful voice.
He has burst his three days' prison;
Let the whole wide earth rejoice.
Death is conquered; man is free.
Christ has won the victory!

As one of His *special witnesses* on earth today, this glorious Easter Sunday, I declare that this is true.[16]

I rejoice in the flood of light that flows from the scriptures and from the teachings and testimonies of prophets, seers, and revelators and special witnesses, ancient (see Acts 1:21–22; 10:40–43) and modern, who teach us of the meaning and eternal significance of Easter—the Lord's Day—and who bear witness of the divinity and living reality of the Lord Jesus Christ!

I too know and bear witness that Jesus is the Christ, the Son of the Living God. He is the Savior and Redeemer of the world. I know and bear witness that He who was crucified for the sins of the world came forth triumphant from the tomb with a body of flesh and bones on that first Easter morning. I know and bear witness that the Resurrection of the Lord Jesus Christ was the great crowning event of His life and mission and that it was the capstone of the Atonement. I know and bear witness that the Atonement is not *part* of the gospel—"the Atonement is the Gospel,"[17] as declared in the Doctrine and Covenants: "And this is the gospel, the glad tidings, which the voice out of the heavens bore record unto us—that he came into the world, even Jesus, to be crucified for the world, and to bear the sins of the world, and to sanctify the world, and to cleanse it from all unrighteousness; that through him all might be saved" (D&C 76:40–42).

And I know and bear witness that through the Atonement of Christ, we and all mankind can be saved by obedience to the laws and ordinances of the gospel, including the ordinances of the holy temple, which make it possible for us not only to enjoy glorious reunions with those who have gone before but to live forever as families in the presence of God! Of these things I humbly testify in the name of Jesus Christ, amen.

NOTES

1. Gordon B. Hinckley, "This Glorious Easter Morn," *Ensign*, May 1996, 66; emphasis added.
2. Gordon B. Hinckley, in "Special Witnesses of Christ," *Ensign*, April 2001, 4; emphasis added.
3. Hinckley, in "Special Witnesses of Christ," 4.
4. See Matthew 16:21; 17:22–23; Luke 24:5–7; emphasis added.
5. Hinckley, "This Glorious Easter Morn," 66.
6. Hinckley, in "Special Witnesses of Christ," 14–15.
7. Hinckley, in "Special Witnesses of Christ," 15.
8. Hinckley, "This Glorious Easter Morn," 66.
9. Hinckley, in "Special Witnesses of Christ," 15.
10. Hinckley, in "Special Witnesses of Christ," 15.
11. Bruce R. McConkie, *Mormon Doctrine*, 2nd ed. (Salt Lake City: Bookcraft, 1979), 658.
12. McConkie, *Mormon Doctrine*, 658.
13. James E. Talmage, *Jesus the Christ* (Salt Lake City: Deseret Book, 1973), 689.
14. Talmage, *Jesus the Christ*, 690.
15. Hinckley, "This Glorious Easter Morn," 67; emphasis added.
16. Thomas S. Monson, "He Is Risen!," *Ensign*, May 2010, 89–90; emphasis added.
17. McConkie, *Mormon Doctrine*, 60.

Because of his death on the cross, we can celebrate the
grace of his Atonement; we can rejoice in God's great
love for us that he would give his Only Begotten Son.

(Carl Bloch, *The Crucifixion*, © Intellectual Reserve, Inc.)

Christ's Crucifixion
Reclamation of the Cross

Gaye Strathearn

TWENTY-THREE YEARS AGO, I came to BYU as a student. This was a major, life-changing event for me. My mother and grandmother had joined the Church in Australia in 1958, and I spent most of my early life growing up in a *very* small branch of the Church, small even by Australian standards. You can perhaps imagine my feelings of excitement at the thought of coming to live in the heartland of the Church. It was quite a novel thought that I would be able to go to Church with my roommates. I still remember my feelings of wonderment and excitement as I walked to the Marriott Center for my first devotional along with thousands of people my

Gaye Strathearn is an associate professor of ancient scripture at Brigham Young University.

age as the carillon bell played "Come, Come, Ye Saints"! Against the backdrop of such wonderment, it was a huge culture shock for me when Easter came and I realized that Good Friday was a nonevent at BYU. Honestly, I was quite surprised that it was business as usual with classes being held on what I considered to be one of the holiest days in the Christian calendar.

While I know that it isn't true, there is a part of me that can understand how an outsider might form the following conclusion that was published in an issue of the *Newsweek* magazine: "Mormons do not . . . place much emphasis on Easter."[1]

I have been asked to speak on "Christ's Crucifixion: The Reclamation of the Cross." Before turning to this subject, I would like to make two caveat statements. First, I want to say that the nature of my topic means that I will not be discussing much about Gethsemane. Even so, I want to make it clear that I recognize that the events that took place in the Garden of Gethsemane are absolutely seminal to our understanding of the Atonement. Second, I want to be clear that in this paper I am *not* advocating that the Church should start putting up crosses on our chapels or temples. That is certainly *not* my place. What I do want to argue, however, is that if we fail to appreciate or if we minimize the importance of the cross and what it stands for, then we ignore a very significant part of our scriptural texts: both in the Bible *and* in our Restoration scriptures, the Book of Mormon and the Doctrine and Covenants.

So with that in mind, I will begin by reviewing some of the historical details of crucifixion in antiquity, including what pagans thought about the fact that Christians worshipped a god that had been crucified and how the Apostle Paul countered such arguments. Then I will suggest four reasons why I believe that the cross today should play an important part in our study and both our private and public discourse.

CRUCIFIXION: "A MOST MISERABLE DEATH"

Although each emphasizes its own unique aspects, all four Gospels are united in their witness that Jesus was crucified on a cross. Matthew, Mark, and John call the site of the Crucifixion Golgotha (see Matthew 27:33; Mark 15:22; John 19:17). Luke uses the Latin term *Calvary* (see Luke 23:33).

The Jewish historian Josephus described crucifixion as "the most pitiable of deaths" (*thanatōn ton oiktiston*).[2] Crucifixion was an ugly way to die—purposely so. Although it is generally acknowledged that the Persians invented crucifixion,[3] the reality is that many ancient groups practiced it[4] and that it was performed in different ways.[5] Sometimes it meant that the victims were impaled (*anestaurōse*);[6] sometimes they were tied to a cross or a tree,[7] but usually they were nailed.[8] Archaeologically, only one set of remains has been found of a person who was crucified in Palestine prior to AD 70. We know that the person was crucified because the nail was still in the right calcaneum (or heel bone). These remains suggest that in this case the individual's feet were nailed on either side of the vertical pole.[9] Often the victims were crucified while alive, but sometimes it was after they were dead.[10] Sometimes the victim was even crucified upside down.[11] Sometimes the legs were broken in conjunction with the crucifixion.[12] By Roman times, crucifixion was preceded by flogging,[13] and the victims "often carried the beam to the place of execution, where [they were] nailed to it with outstretched arms, raised up and seated on a small wooden peg."[14] Sometimes the bodies were left to be devoured by birds and wild animals,[15] but in Roman times

A representation of what the nails may have looked like.
(Matt Reier, *Nails*, © Intellectual Reserve, Inc.)

it was possible for the family to petition to take the body and bury it once death had been verified.[16] Crucifixion was chosen as a form of execution, especially for murderers, thieves, traitors, and slaves, because it was public and humiliating, and because the torture could be extended for long periods of time.[17] One first-century Roman author named Quintilian wrote, "When we crucify criminals the most frequented roads are chosen, where the greatest number of people can look and be seized by this fear. For every punishment has less to do with the offence than with the example."[18]

The accounts of Jesus' Crucifixion in the four Gospels are the most detailed accounts that we have of an ancient crucifixion. Many, but not all, of the points noted in the gospel are known details from ancient sources that we have discussed above. Prior to crucifixion, Jesus was scourged (see Mark 15:15) and forced to carry his cross, although Simon of Cyrene did it for him (see Matthew 27:32). The soldiers also gave Jesus a drink of gall and vinegar (see v. 34). In the gospel accounts of the Crucifixion, there is no specific mention of Jesus being nailed to the cross, although, as we have noted, that was the usual practice, as is indicated in Jesus' case by Thomas's exclamation, "Except I shall see in his hands the print of the nails, and put my finger into the print of the nails, and thrust my hand into his side, I will not believe" (John 20:25). A sign reading "The King of the Jews" was placed on the cross (Mark 15:26; Matthew 27:37; Luke 23:38;

John 19:19), and passersby mocked him (see Matthew 27:39–43). The soldiers would have broken his legs to hasten his death before the beginning of the Sabbath, but he was already dead (see John 19:32–33),[19] and Joseph of Arimathea petitioned Pilate to be able to bury Jesus' body (see Luke 23:50–53).

But while the Gospels describe the Crucifixion in terms of what happened, and Acts shows that the Crucifixion was at the heart of the teachings of Peter and John (see Acts 2:23, 36; 4:10), it is only the writings of Paul that discuss the *why* of Christ's Crucifixion. At least some early Christians seemed to struggle with the idea that the Son of God would be executed in such a shameful manner as crucifixion. Paul acknowledged to the Galatians that under the law of Moses, "cursed is every one that hangeth on a tree" (Galatians 3:13; see also Deuteronomy 21:22–23).[20]

We also know that pagans mocked Christians for worshipping a God who was crucified. One example is the second-century Cynic philosopher Lucian, who once lived among Christians in Palestine. He later wrote a satire that mocked Christians who "have sinned by denying the Greek gods, and by worshipping that crucified sophist himself and living according to his laws." Further, he was a man "whom they still worship—the man who was crucified in Palestine for introducing this new cult into the world."[21] In the literature, we also see Christians and pagans in dialogue over the value of the Crucifixion. In the second century, Justin Martyr, a Christian apologist, identified the charges and responded to them: "It is for this that they charge us with madness, saying that we give the second place after the unchanging and ever-existing God and begetter of all things to a crucified man."[22] In the second or third century, in Minucius Felix's *Octavius,* we read a pagan quip against Christians: "To say that a malefactor put to death for his crimes, and wood of the death-dealing cross, are objects of their veneration is to assign fitting altars to abandoned wretches and the kind of worship they deserve."[23] A graphic representation of the disdain that pagans had for the Christian worship of a crucified god may be a graffito carved into plaster on a wall near the Palentine Hill in Rome that is probably dated from the second or third century.[24] It depicts a boy at the foot of a crucified man that has the head of a donkey. The crude inscription reads, "Alexamenos, worship [your] God."[25]

It is this type of criticism of Christianity, "the offence [Greek *skandalon*] of the cross" (Galatians 5:11), that Paul is probably responding to as he emphasizes the importance of the cross. He acknowledges this type of taunt when he declares, "For the preaching of the cross is to them that perish foolishness; but unto us which are saved it is the power of God. . . . For the Jews require a sign, and the Greeks seek after wisdom: but we preach Christ crucified, unto the Jews a stumbling-block, and unto the Greeks foolishness" (1 Corinthians 1:18, 22–23). Not only is the crucified Christ not foolishness to Paul, it is in fact the *power of God.*

Therefore, Paul asserts the centrality of this message for his missionary activities: "For I determined not to know any thing among you, save Jesus Christ, and him crucified" (1 Corinthians 2:2). Later, in a response to Christians in Corinth who were rejecting the reality and importance of the Resurrection, he makes a statement that in our English King James Bible loses some of its impact: "For I delivered unto you first of all that which I also received, how that Christ died for our sins according to the scriptures; and that he was buried, and that he rose again the third day according to the scriptures" (1 Corinthians 15:3–4). The phrase in Greek that is translated as "first of all" is *en prōtois*, which can be more accurately translated as "most important."[26] In other words, Paul taught that *the most important things* that he had delivered unto them were (1) the Crucifixion and (2) the Resurrection. In his mind, the Crucifixion, rather than being an embarrassment, was in fact *central* to his missionary message.

In the second century, Justin Martyr would argue that the Crucifixion, a point of ridicule for pagans, was in fact the very thing that separated Christianity from all other religions.[27]

WHY SHOULD THE CROSS BE MEANINGFUL TO LATTER-DAY SAINTS?

As I have thought about Christ's Crucifixion and the central place that Good Friday has held historically and theologically in Christianity, I would like to discuss four reasons why I believe that the cross should hold an important place in our private and public discourse, both among ourselves and in conjunction with our Christian friends.[28]

1. *The events on the cross are an integral part of the Atonement.* The most important reason that we should consider the cross is that both doctrinally and functionally it is part of Christ's Atonement. I think it is fair to say that traditionally Latter-day Saints have emphasized the Atonement as taking part in Gethsemane. For example, Elder Bruce R. McConkie has written:

> Where and under what circumstances was the atoning sacrifice of the Son of God made? Was it on the Cross of Calvary or in the Garden of Gethsemane? It is to the Cross of Christ that most Christians look when centering their attention upon the infinite and eternal atonement. And certainly the sacrifice of our Lord was completed when he was lifted up by men; also, that part of his life and suffering is more dramatic and, perhaps, more soul stirring. But in reality the pain and suffering, the triumph and grandeur, of the atonement took place primarily in Gethsemane. . . . Many have been crucified and the torment and pain is extreme. But only one, and he the Man who had God as his Father, has bowed beneath the burden of grief and sorrow that lay

upon him in that awful night, that night in which he descended below all things as he prepared himself to rise above them all.[29]

As we have already noted, it is certainly true that many people were crucified in antiquity. At a later time, however, Elder McConkie also taught, "All of the anguish, all of the sorrow, and all of the suffering of Gethsemane recurred during the final three hours on the cross, the hours when darkness covered the land. Truly there was no sorrow like unto his sorrow, and no anguish and pain like unto that which bore in with such intensity upon him."[30] This reality suggests that Christ's Crucifixion was unlike any other's experience. Elder Neal A. Maxwell reminds us of "the axis of agony which was Gethsemane *and* Calvary."[31] Thus Paul taught the Romans that "we were reconciled to God by the death of his Son . . . by whom we have now received the atonement" (Romans 5:10–11).

I am struck by the number of times that the teachings on the Atonement and redemption in the Book of Mormon and the Doctrine and Covenants specifically include Christ's death in the equation.

For the Book of Mormon, the cross is *not* a marginal footnote to the Atonement. Rather, the phrase "sufferings and death" is at the very heart of some important sermons. For example, when Alma the Elder was secretly preaching the words of Abinadi, he taught, "Yea, concerning that which was to come, and also concerning the resurrection of the dead, and the redemption of the people, which was to be brought to pass through the power, and *sufferings, and death of Christ*, and his resurrection and ascension into heaven" (Mosiah 18:2; emphasis added). When Aaron, the son of Mosiah, preached to the Amalekites in the city of Jerusalem, we read, "Now Aaron began to open the scriptures unto them concerning the coming of Christ, and also concerning the resurrection of the dead, and that there could be no redemption for mankind save it were through the *death and sufferings of Christ*, and the atonement of his blood." Likewise, when he preached to King Lamoni's father, Aaron declared, "And since man had fallen he could not merit anything of himself; but the *sufferings and death of Christ* atone for their sins" (Alma 22:14; emphasis added). Finally, when Mormon wrote to his son Moroni, he implored that Christ's "sufferings and death . . . rest in your mind forever" (Moroni 9:25).

In the Doctrine and Covenants, such as section 19, we find powerful verses about the Atonement in Gethsemane, but we also have verses where redemption is specifically identified with the cross. In sections 53 and 54, Jesus himself declares to both Sidney Gilbert and Newel Knight that he "was crucified for the sins of the world" (D&C 53:2; 54:1), and in the revelation to President Joseph F. Smith on the redemption of the dead we read, "And so it was made known among the dead, both small and great, the unrighteous as well as the faithful, that redemption had been wrought through the sacrifice of the Son of God upon the cross" (D&C 138:35).

All of these passages from our Restoration scripture support the biblical message of Paul that the Crucifixion of our Lord was an essential part of the Atonement, and thus that it is an essential part of our personal and collective redemption. Elder Holland described Easter Friday as "atoning Friday with its cross."[32] I like that description because it reminds me of why Easter Friday should be an important part of the Easter season.

2. *The scriptural metaphor that we can be "lifted up" because Christ was lifted up on the cross is a symbol of God's great love for us.* On day two of the Savior's visit to the Americas, he responded to a request from his disciples, "Tell us the name whereby we shall call this church" (3 Nephi 27:3). Jesus responded with two qualifications for the Church: it must bear his name, and it must be "built upon [his] gospel" (vv. 5–10). Then he proceeded to do something that we have no record of him doing in biblical times; in the following verses he gives a definition of his gospel:

> Behold I have given unto you my gospel, and this is the gospel which I have given unto you—that I came into the world to do the will of my Father, because my Father sent me.

And my Father sent me that I might be lifted up upon the cross; and after that I had been lifted up upon the cross, that I might draw all men unto me, that as I have been lifted up by men even so should men be lifted up by the Father, to stand before me, to be judged of their works, whether they be good or whether they be evil—

And for this cause have I been lifted up; therefore, according to the power of the Father I will draw all men unto me, that they may be judged according to their works. (vv. 13–15)

What is important for our discussion is that when the Savior himself describes his gospel and the Atonement, he describes it in terms of the cross: "My Father sent me that I might be lifted up on the cross" (v. 14). Notice the purpose of Christ being lifted up on the cross: so that he could draw all men unto him to be judged.[33] Then the rest of his definition of the gospel outlines what we must do to make sure that day of judgment is a day of rejoicing: we must repent, be baptized in his name, endure to the end, and be sanctified by the Holy Ghost "that [we] may stand spotless before [him] at the last day" (v. 20).

Although in this passage being "lifted up" is associated with judgment, in other places it is associated with God's great love for his people. For example, when Jesus spoke with Nicodemus, he made reference to Moses lifting up a brass serpent to heal the Israelites who had been infiltrated by a plague of serpents. Jesus specifically identified the act of raising a pole with a serpent as a type of his Crucifixion: "And as Moses lifted up the serpent in the wilderness, even so must the Son of man be lifted up: that whosoever believeth in him should not perish, but have eternal life" (John 3:14–15). Then note the famous verses that immediately follow: "For God so loved the world, that he gave his only begotten Son, that whosoever believeth in him should not perish, but have everlasting life. For God sent not his Son into the world to condemn the world; but that the world through him might be saved" (vv. 16–17). The context of this passage indicates that the evidence of God's great love for the world is that his Son was lifted up on the cross so that everyone could have eternal life.

This same principle is also found in Nephi's vision of the tree of life. Nephi learns that the tree represents "the love of God, which sheddeth itself abroad in the hearts of the children of men; wherefore, it is most desirable above all things" (1 Nephi 11:22). Then the heavens are opened to Nephi, and he sees in a vision the manifestations of that love: he sees the mortal ministry of the Son of God, John the Baptist and Jesus' baptism, the Twelve Apostles, angels ministering to the people, and Jesus healing the sick. And then we read: "And it came to pass that the angel spake unto me again, saying: Look! And I looked and beheld the Lamb of God, that he was taken by the people; yea, the Son of the everlasting God was judged of the world; and I saw and bear record. And I, Nephi, saw that he was lifted up upon the cross for the sins of the world" (vv. 32–33). Again, the context of this chapter reinforces Jesus' teachings to Nicodemus: Jesus' being lifted up upon the cross was a manifestation of the love of God.

The phrase "lifted up" thus becomes in the scriptures a frequent way to describe salvation. Nephi teaches his brothers, "The righteous have I justified, and testified that they should be lifted up at the last day" (1 Nephi 16:2). In the Doctrine and Covenants we find this image used frequently. The Lord tells Martin Harris, "And if thou art faithful in keeping my commandments, thou shalt be lifted up at the last day" (D&C 5:35). Oliver Cowdery is instructed, "Stand fast in the work wherewith I have called you, and a hair of your head shall not be lost, and you shall be lifted up at the last day" (D&C 9:14). Likewise, the Three Witnesses, Oliver Cowdery, David Whitmer, and Martin Harris, are all promised, "And if you do these last commandments of mine, which I have given you, the gates of hell shall not prevail against you; for my grace is sufficient for you, and you shall be lifted up at the last day" (D&C 17:8).

3. *In the New Testament the invitation to take up our cross was* the *symbol of discipleship.* In the synoptic Gospels, just after Jesus had promised Peter that he would give to him the sealing keys, Jesus began to speak openly about his destiny to go to Jerusalem,

where he would "suffer many things of the elders and chief priests and scribes, and be killed, and be raised again the third day" (Matthew 16:21; see Mark 8:31; Luke 9:22). Peter immediately tried to assure his Master that this would not happen, to which Jesus responded by saying, "Get thee behind me, Satan: thou art an offence unto me: for thou savourest not the things that be of God, but those that be of men. Then said Jesus unto his disciples, If any man will come after me, let him deny himself, and take up his cross, and follow me" (Matthew 16:23–24). Luke, who uses a slightly different form of the verb (*arneomai*), adds, "Let him deny himself, and take up his cross *daily*, and follow me (Luke 9:23; emphasis added). What does it mean for us to "take up our cross"? In the context of these passages it means to deny ourselves. Both Matthew and Mark use the Greek word *aparneomai*. It suggests that discipleship entails the breaking of every link that ties a person even to themselves. It is about being able, like the Savior, to submit our will to the will of the Father. As Elder Maxwell taught, it is "really the only uniquely personal thing we have to place on God's altar."[34] Just as there was a cost for the Savior on Calvary, there is also a cost to be a disciple. In fact, in other settings, Jesus also taught, "And he that taketh *not* his cross, and followeth after me, *is not worthy of me*" (Matthew 10:38; emphasis added), and even more pointedly, "Whosoever doth not bear his cross, and come after me, *cannot* be my disciple" (Luke 14:27; emphasis added).

Paul understood something of the cost of being a disciple. He acknowledged to the Philippians, "But what things were gain to me, those I counted loss for Christ . . . that I may know him, and the power of his resurrection, and the fellowship of his sufferings, being made conformable unto his death [i.e., to be like Christ in his death; Greek *summorphizō*]" (Philippians 3:7, 10). More specifically, he declared to the Galatians, "I have been crucified with Christ." For him, crucifixion was a symbol not of death but of life, a new life in Christ. "Nevertheless I live; yet not I, but Christ liveth in me: and the life which I now live in the flesh I live by the faith of the Son of God, who loved me, and gave himself for me" (Galatians 2:20). "But God forbid that I should glory, save in the cross of our Lord Jesus Christ, by whom the world is crucified unto me, and I unto the world" (Galatians 6:14).

Thus the symbol of the cross is *not* a postbiblical symbol adopted by Christians; rather it is a symbol identified by the Savior himself, and emphasized by Paul. The symbol of the cross is important because in the New Testament it is *the* symbol of our discipleship and commitment to leave behind the allurements of the world and dedicate ourselves to the Lord and his kingdom.

4. The signs of the Crucifixion were so important for Christ that he kept them even after he received a glorified, resurrected body. When Jesus first came to the temple in Bountiful, the people were not initially sure who appeared to them. Even though, after the third time, they finally understood the words of the Father, "Behold my Beloved Son, in whom I am well pleased, in whom I have glorified my name—hear ye him," when they saw Jesus descending out of heaven and standing in the midst of them, "they thought it was an angel that had appeared unto them" (3 Nephi 11:7–8). So Jesus declared to them:

> Behold, I am Jesus Christ, whom the prophets testified shall come into the world.
>
> And behold, I am the light and the life of the world; and I have drunk out of that bitter cup which the Father hath given me, and have glorified the Father in taking upon me the sins of the world, in the which I have suffered the will of the Father in all things from the beginning. . . .
>
> Arise and come forth unto me, that ye may thrust your hands into my side, and also that ye may feel the prints of the nails in my hands and in my feet, that ye may know that I am the God of Israel, and the God of the whole earth, and have been slain for the sins of the world." (vv. 10–11, 14)

Here stood the Son of God in a glorified, resurrected body; a body that was perfect in every way, except for the fact that, as prophesied by Zechariah (see Zechariah 13:6), he chose to retain the marks of

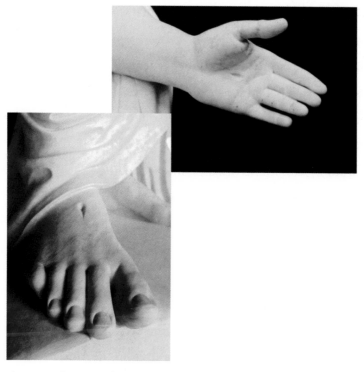

The signs of the Crucifixion did not cause
mourning but were a reason to rejoice!

his Crucifixion. For the people of 3 Nephi, this retention was one of
the tangible proofs that this being was not an angel but was in fact
the Savior of the world. And after they each went forth one by one
and "thrust their hands into his side, and did feel the prints of the
nails in his hands and in his feet. . . . They did cry out with one ac-
cord, saying: Hosanna! Blessed be the name of the Most High God!
And they did fall down at the feet of Jesus, and did worship him"
(3 Nephi 11:15–17).

I wonder how many of those present at that supernal time might have remembered what Jehovah had said to the prophet Isaiah, and what had been recorded in the Nephite records: "Can a woman forget her sucking child, that she should not have compassion on the son of her womb? yea, they may forget, yet will I not forget thee. Behold, I have graven thee upon the palms of my hands" (Isaiah 49:15–16; 1 Nephi 21:16). In this instance, the signs of the Crucifixion did not cause mourning but were a reason to rejoice!

Finally, Elder Holland gives us another reason to rejoice in the signs of the Crucifixion that Christ retained in his resurrected body:

> When we stagger or stumble, He is there to steady and strengthen us. In the end He is there to save us, and for all this He gave His life. However dim our days may seem, they have been a lot darker for the Savior of the world. As a reminder of those days, Jesus has chosen, even in a resurrected, otherwise perfected body, to retain for the benefit of His disciples the wounds in His hands and in His feet and in His side—signs, if you will, that painful things happen even to the pure and the perfect; signs, if you will, that pain in this world is *not* evidence that God doesn't love you; signs, if you will, that problems pass and happiness can be ours. . . . It is the wounded Christ who is the Captain of our souls, He who yet bears the scars of

our forgiveness, the lesions of His love and humility, the torn flesh of obedience and sacrifice. These wounds are the principal way we are to recognize Him when He comes.[35]

CONCLUSION

Most of the Christian world refers to Easter Friday as Good Friday. This may seem odd for a day that commemorates death, even the cruel, torturous death of the Son of God. It is called Good Friday because the word *good* in English can mean "pious or holy." In that sense, Good Friday is a most holy day. But in spite of sordid details of the way Jesus was crucified, I hope that during the Easter season we will find reason to rejoice and celebrate his death as well as his Resurrection. Because of his death on the cross, we can celebrate the grace of his Atonement; we can rejoice in God's great love for us that he would give his Only Begotten Son; we can celebrate the opportunity to respond to Jesus' invitation for all to come, follow him, and be his disciples; and in our darkest moments, we can find solace and reason to rejoice in the memory that we are engraven in the palms of his hands! I thank God for *all* of the Easter season.

NOTES

1. Kenneth L. Woodward, "What Mormons Believe," *Newsweek*, September 1, 1980, 70.
2. Josephus, *The Jewish War* (1928; repr., Cambridge, MA: Harvard University Press, 1968) 7.203.

3. J. Schneider, "σταυρός," in *Theological Dictionary of the New Testament*, ed. Gerhard Friedrich (Grand Rapids, MI: Eerdmans, 1971), 7:573.

4. Martin Hengel, *Crucifixion in the Ancient World and the Folly of the Message of the Cross* (Philadelphia: Fortress, 1977), 22–23.

5. "The soldiers out of rage and hatred amused themselves by nailing their prisoners in different postures; and so great was their number, that space could not be found for the crosses nor crosses for the bodies." Josephus, *Jewish War* 5.451. "Yonder I see instruments of torture [crosses; *cruces* in Latin], not indeed of a single kind, but differently contrived by different peoples; some hang their victims with head toward the ground, some impale their private parts, others stretch out their arms on a fork-shaped gibbet." Seneca, *Dialogue: De Consolatione ad Marciam* (1932; repr., Cambridge, MA: Harvard University Press, 1965) 20.3.

6. Herodotus, *History* (1921; repr., Cambridge, MA: Harvard University Press, 1971) 3.125.3; Polybius, *Histories* (1923; repr., Cambridge, MA: Harvard University Press, 2011) 8.21.

7. Galatians 3:13; 11Q19 64.9–11. The apocryphal *Acts of Andrew* describes Andrew's crucifixion: "They . . . bound his feet and his arm-pits, without nailing him." Wilhelm Schneemelcher, ed., *New Testament Apocrypha*, trans. R. McL. Wilson (Louisville: Westminster/John Knox, 1992), 2:148.

8. Kent P. Jackson, "The Crucifixion," in *From the Last Supper through the Resurrection: The Savior's Final Hours*, ed. Richard Neitzel Holzapfel and Thomas A. Wayment (Salt Lake City: Deseret Book, 2003), 320n7. See also Josephus, *Jewish War* 2.308; 5.451.

9. Joe Zias and James H. Charlesworth, "Crucifixion: Archaeology, Jesus, and the Dead Sea Scrolls," in *Jesus and the Dead Sea Scrolls*, ed. James H. Charlesworth (New York: Doubleday, 1992), 279–80. See also Herodotus, *History* 9.120; Josephus, *Jewish War* 5.451.

10. "They were accordingly scourged and subjected to torture of every description, before being killed, and then crucified opposite the walls." Josephus, *Jewish War* 5.449.

11. Seneca, *Dialogue: De Consolatione ad Marciam* 20.3. See text in note 5.

12. Cicero, *Philippics* (Cambridge, MA: Harvard University Press, 2009) 13.27.

13. See Josephus, *Antiquities of the Jews* (1943; repr., Cambridge, MA: Harvard University Press, 1966) 12.255–56; Josephus, *Jewish War* 2.307; Philo, *Flaccus* 10.84. English translation from *The Works of Philo: Complete and Unabridged, New Updated Version*, trans. C. D. Yonge (Peabody, MA: Hendrickson, 1992).

14. Hengel, *Crucifixion in the Ancient World*, 25. For an example of having to carry the cross beam, see Plutarch, "On the Delays of Divine Vengeance," *Moralia* (1959; repr., Cambridge, MA: Harvard University Press, 1968) 7:554 A, B.

15. Juvenal, *Satire* (Cambridge, MA: Harvard University Press, 2004) 14.77–78; *Acts of Andrew,* in Schneemelcher, *New Testament Apocrypha*, 148.

16. "The bodies of those who suffer capital punishment are not to be refused to their relatives; and the deified Augustus writes in the tenth book of his *de Vita Sua* that he also had observed this [custom]. Today, however, the bodies of those who are executed are buried in the same manner as if this had been sought and granted. But sometimes it is not allowed, particularly [with the bodies] of those condemned for treason. . . . The bodies of executed persons are to be granted to any who seek them for burial." Corpus Iuris Civilis, *Pandectae* 48.24.1–3; English translation in *The Digest of Justinian*, ed. Theodor Mommsen and Paul Krueger, trans. Alan Watson (Philadelphia: University of Pennsylvania Press, 1985), 4:863. In the Dead Sea Scrolls *Temple Scroll* it was forbidden that corpses be left on a tree overnight (11Q19 64.11–13). "I have known of instances before now of men who had been crucified when this festival and holiday [i.e., the Emperor's birthday] was at hand, being taken down and given up to their relations, in order to receive the honours of sepulture, and to enjoy such observances as are due to the dead." Philo, *Flaccus* 10.83.

17. For excellent LDS discussions on crucifixion, see Jackson, "The Crucifixion," 318–37; Donald W. Parry and Jay A. Parry, "The Cruel Cross: The Crucifixion," in *Symbols and Shadows: Unlocking a Deeper Understanding of the Atonement* (Salt Lake City: Deseret Book, 2009), 222–53.

18. Quintilian, *Declamations* 274.13. English translation in *Quintilian: The Lesser Declamations*, ed. and trans. D. R. Shackleton Bailey (Cambridge,

MA: Harvard University Press, 2006), 1:259.

19. Erkki Koskenniemi, Kirsi Nisula, and Jorma Toppari, "Wine Mixed with Myrrh (Mark 15.23) and Crurifragium (John 19.31–32): Two Details of the Passion Narratives," *Journal for the Study of the New Testament* 27, no. 4 (2005): 279–91.

20. Tertullian responds to this Jewish complaint in *An Answer to the Jews*, trans. S. Thelwall (New York: Kessinger, 2004), 164.

21. Lucian, *The Death of Peregrinus*, 13, 11, in *Lucian: Selected Dialogues*, trans. Desmond Costa (Oxford: Oxford University Press, 2005), 77.

22. Justin Martyr, *First Apology of Justin* 1.13.4, in *Early Christian Fathers*, ed. and trans. Cyril C. Richardson (New York: Collier Books, Macmillan, 1970), 249.

23. Minucius Felix, *Octavius* (1931; repr., Cambridge, MA: Harvard University Press, 1984) 9.4.

24. George M. A. Hanfmann, "The Crucified Donkey Man: Achaios and Jesus," in *Studies in Classical Art and Archaeology: A Tribute to Peter Heinrich von Blanckenhagen*, ed. Günter Kopcke and Mary B. Moore (Locust Valley, NY: J. J. Augustin, 1979), 205–7, pl. 55, 1.2; Peter Lampe, *From Paul to Valentinus: Christians at Rome in the First Two Centuries*, trans. Michael Steinhauser, ed. Marshall D. Johnson (Minneapolis: Fortress Press, 2003), 338; G. H. R. Horsley, *New Documents Illustrating Early Christianity: A Review of the Greek Inscriptions and Papyri Published in 1979* (North Ryde, NSW: Ancient History Documentary Research Centre, Macquarie University, 1987), 137.

25. The charge that Christians worshipped a god with an ass's head is one that early Christian writers had to deal with. For example, see Tertullian, *To the Nations* (Peabody, MA: Hendrickson, 1994), 11, 14; and Minucius Felix, *Octavius* 9.3. Jews also had to deal with this type of charge. Josephus recounts that Apion claimed a man by the name of Zabidus entered their temple and "snatched up the golden head of the pack-ass." Josephus shows his disdain for the account by inserting the comment "as he facetiously calls it." Josephus, *Against Apion* (Cambridge, MA: Harvard University Press) 2.114.

26. "πρῶτος," in *A Greek-English Lexicon of the New Testament and Other Early Christian Literature*, ed. William F. Arndt and F. Wilbur Gingrich, 2nd ed. (Chicago: University of Chicago Press, 1958), 726.

27. Justin Martyr, *First Apology of Justin* 1.13.4 and 55.1, 249, 278.

28. For another discussion of Latter-day Saint teachings on the cross, see Robert L. Millet, *What Happened to the Cross? Distinctive LDS Teachings* (Salt Lake City: Deseret Book, 2007), 96–114.

29. Bruce R. McConkie, *Doctrinal New Testament Commentary* (Salt Lake City: Bookcraft, 1979), 1:774–75.

30. Bruce R. McConkie, *The Mortal Messiah* (Salt Lake City: Deseret Book, 1981), 4:232n22.

31. Neal A. Maxwell, "'Apply the Atoning Blood of Christ,'" *Ensign*, November 1997, 23; emphasis added.

32. Jeffrey R. Holland, "None Were with Him," *Ensign*, May 2009, 88.

33. Compare John 12:32–33, where Jesus says, "And I, if I be lifted up from the earth, will draw all men unto me. This he said, signifying what death he should die."

34. Neal A. Maxwell, "'Swallowed Up in the Will of the Father,'" *Ensign*, November 1995, 24.

35. Jeffrey R. Holland, "Teaching, Preaching, Healing," *Ensign*, January 2003, 42.

Moments after Jesus breathed his last breath, the environment and atmosphere of his torturous, abusive, pitied, and ignominious Crucifixion changed abruptly and completely. Though his physical body died, his spirit body continued to live—as will each of ours—and Jesus entered the world of spirits.

(Robert Barrett, *Christ Teaching in the Spirit World*, © Intellectual Reserve, Inc.)

THE SAVIOR'S MINISTRY TO THE SPIRIT WORLD

Andrew C. Skinner

A T ABOUT THREE o'clock on a Friday afternoon, in a then-
obscure province of the eastern Roman Empire almost two
thousand years ago, Jesus of Nazareth drew his last labored breath
in mortality. The minutes *before* his decease and the minutes *after*
are a study in contrasts. And this is one of two focal points for
our part of the story—a story encompassing what Hugh Nibley
called the "three missions," the "three descents" of Christ. The
first was "as a mortal condescending to mortals"; the second "as
a spirit, ministering to spirits in their deep prison"; and the third
"as a glorified, resurrected being who frequently descends . . .

---

*Andrew C. Skinner is a professor of ancient
scripture at Brigham Young University.*

to minister to certain mortals who share in his glory in special manifestations."[1]

As Jesus hung on the cruel cross of crucifixion, nailed to its wood by iron spikes hammered in by expert crucifiers, the physical and spiritual pain, the agony, the torture so intense as to be incomprehensible to finite minds, reached a crescendo. God the Father completely withdrew his support and caused an agony of soul so great as to elicit a cry of abandonment from Jesus (see Matthew 27:46; Mark 15:34). But this withdrawal was the only way Jesus could die, since the Father's spirit and influence are life-giving and life-sustaining. If the Father had not withdrawn from the Son again on the cross as he did in Gethsemane, Jesus would have been sustained and nourished by the light and life of his Father's spirit. Total degeneration of his body could not have occurred, and thus he could not have died so readily by an act of will. One writer has noted, "The withdrawal of the Spirit from Jesus, with the influence which the powers of spiritual death and darkness then had upon Him, apparently caused a critical breakdown to occur in His bodily organs and tissues so that, when He willed that He should die, His spirit could readily depart into the spirit world."[2]

What added to the utterly pathetic atmosphere of this crucifixion scene were the taunts, the mockings, the jeers, and the undeserved abuse heaped upon Jesus by passersby who did not know, understand, or care about the true significance of the events that were unfolding before their very eyes. Matthew reports, "They that passed by reviled him, wagging their heads, and saying, Thou that destroy-est the temple, and buildest it in three days, save thyself. If thou be the Son of God, come down from the cross" (Matthew 27:39–40). Luke similarly records, "The people stood beholding. And the rulers also with them derided him. . . . And the soldiers also mocked him" (Luke 23:35–36).

Stunningly, *all* this was captured by the Psalmist many centuries before it happened.

> "My God, my God, why hast thou forsaken me? why art thou so far from helping me, and from the words of my roaring?" (Psalm 22:1; compare Matthew 27:46; Mark 15:34)

> "All they that see me laugh me to scorn: they shoot out the lip, they shake the head." (Psalm 22:7; compare Matthew 27:39; Mark 15:29; Luke 23:35)

> The scorners said, "He trusted on the Lord that he would deliver him: let him deliver him, seeing he delighted in him." (Psalm 22:8; compare Matthew 27:43)

> "I am poured out like water, and all my bones are out of joint: my heart is like wax; it is melted in the midst of

When Jesus was crucified, except for a relatively small percentage of the population in Judea, Samaria, and Galilee, almost all of the known world had no idea about what was going on at a place called Golgotha. (James Tissot, *The People, Beholding the Things That Were Done, Smote Their Breasts,* © Intellectual Reserve, Inc.)

my bowels. My strength is dried up like a potsherd; and my tongue cleaveth to my jaws; and thou hast brought me into the dust of death." (Psalm 22:14–15; compare John 19:28–29)

"The assembly of the wicked have inclosed me: they pierced my hands and my feet.... They look and stare upon me." (Psalm 22:16–17; compare Matthew 27:35–38)

Furthermore, when Jesus was crucified, except for a relatively small percentage of the population in Judea, Samaria, and Galilee, almost all of the known world had no idea about what was going on at a place called Golgotha. At that moment it was an obscure event. In fact, the term *Golgotha* itself is found in no other ancient, non-Christian records.

On that Friday afternoon, Jesus suffered on the cross until all the things which God the Father desired, and which the demands of justice required, had been accomplished. Then, knowing by revelation that he had fulfilled these things, Jesus uttered the last of his seven statements from the cross—not as it is reported in the King James Version but rather as given in the Joseph Smith Translation: "Jesus, when he had cried again with a loud voice, *saying, Father, it is finished, thy will is done*, yielded up the ghost" (JST, Matthew 27:54; italics show JST change).

The cause of Jesus' physical death in relationship to the horrifying practices of crucifixion has been much discussed. The insight that has come to mean the most to me was offered years ago by Elder James E. Talmage. In sum, he said that he believed Jesus died of a broken heart:

> While, as stated in the text, the yielding up of life was voluntary on the part of Jesus Christ, for He had life in Himself and no man could take His life except as He willed to allow it to be taken, (John 1:4; 5:26; 10:15–18) there was of necessity a direct physical cause of dissolution. . . .

Elder James E. Talmage
(© Intellectual Reserve, Inc.)

The crucified sometimes lived for days upon the cross, and death resulted, not from the infliction of mortal wounds, but from internal congestion, inflammations, organic disturbances, and consequent exhaustion of vital energy. Jesus, though weakened by long torture during the preceding night and early morning, by the shock of the crucifixion itself, as also by intense mental agony, and particularly through spiritual suffering such as no other man has ever endured, manifested surprising vigor, both of mind and body, to the last. The strong, loud utterance, immediately following which He bowed His head and "gave up the ghost," when considered in connection with other recorded details, points to a physical rupture of the heart as the direct cause of death. If the soldier's spear was thrust into the left side of the Lord's body and actually penetrated the heart, the outrush of "blood and water" observed by John is further evidence of a cardiac rupture; for it is known that in the rare instances of death resulting from a breaking of any part of the wall of the heart, blood accumulates within the pericardium, and there undergoes a change by which the corpuscles separate as a partially clotted mass from the almost colorless, watery serum. . . . Great mental stress, poignant emotion either of grief or joy, and intense spiritual struggle are among the recognized causes of heart rupture.

The present writer believes that the Lord Jesus died of a broken heart. The psalmist sang in dolorous measure according to his inspired prevision of the Lord's passion: "Reproach hath broken my heart; and I am full of heaviness: and I looked for some to take pity, but there was none; and for comforters, but I found none. They gave me also gall for my meat; and in my thirst they gave me vinegar to drink" (Ps. 69:20, 21; see also 22:14).[3]

How important to know this, for Jesus asks each of his disciples to offer as a personal sacrifice the very things he suffered in Gethsemane and on the cross—a broken heart and a contrite spirit (see 3 Nephi 9:19–20). According to *Webster's New World Dictionary*, College Edition (1966), a synonym for *contrite* is "crushed."

Moments after Jesus breathed his last breath, the environment and atmosphere of his torturous, abusive, pitied, and ignominious Crucifixion changed abruptly and completely. Though his physical body died, his spirit body continued to live—as will each of ours—and Jesus entered the world of spirits. He did not go to a different planet in some far away place in the universe. Rather, Jesus passed through a veil into a different realm of existence right here on this earth. The spirit world is on this earth. President Brigham Young taught this concept in clarity,[4] as did Elder Parley P. Pratt. In fact, Elder Pratt also implied that the spirit worlds for other earths, like our own, are located on those other planets. Elder Pratt said:

As to its location, [the spirit world] is here on the very planet where we were born; or, in other words, the earth and other planets of a like sphere, have their inward or spiritual spheres, as well as their outward, or temporal.

The one is peopled by temporal tabernacles, and the other by spirits. A vail [*sic*] is drawn between the one sphere and the other, whereby all the objects in the spiritual sphere are rendered invisible to those in the temporal.[5]

The spirit world into which Jesus entered was a fundamentally and thoroughly different environment from the one he had just come from. Let us consider four aspects of comparison. First of all, as the prophet Alma declared "concerning the state of the soul between death and the resurrection" that "the spirits of those who are righteous are received into a state of happiness, which is called paradise, a state of rest, a state of peace, where they shall rest from all their troubles and from all care, and sorrow" (Alma 40:11–12). How unlike the Crucifixion scene was this new condition or state of existence called paradise! The very essence of the former environment (the one at the site of the cross) was sorrow, suffering, excruciating pain, anguish, torture, and horror, while the essence of the latter was (and is) peace, rest, and joyful anticipation (see D&C 138:15).

Second, if there is a single word that might possibly capture the atmosphere that surrounded Jesus at Golgotha, as well as those attitudes about him that were so prevalent on the part of many Jews, perhaps the best word is *ignominy*, meaning shame, dishonor, disgrace, infamy, and contempt—all of which were directed at Jesus. Compare *that* setting with the one of the world of spirits, or at least that portion where Jesus made his personal appearance. "There were gathered together in one place an innumerable company of the spirits of the just. . . . They were filled with joy and gladness, and were rejoicing together because the day of their deliverance was at hand. They were assembled awaiting the advent of the Son of God into the spirit world, to declare their redemption from the bands of death" (D&C 138:12, 15–16).

Third, the number of people at the cross who grasped the significance of Jesus' life and death was very small—if there were any at all. I think the case could be made that even among the Apostles—all but one of whom had forsaken and fled from Jesus (see Matthew 26:56)—there was little real understanding of who Jesus was and what he was doing. As late as the morning of the Resurrection, John records that Peter and he did not know what to make of the empty tomb and missing body of Jesus, "for as yet they knew not the scripture, that he must rise again from the dead" (John 20:9).

On the other hand, compare the language of Doctrine and Covenants 138 in describing those who waited for Jesus, the very God of heaven and earth, to make his appearance. Phrases are used such as "an innumerable company" and a "vast multitude" who were gathered together, "firm in the hope of a glorious resurrection, through the grace of God the Father and his Only Begotten Son, Jesus Christ" (vv. 12, 14, 18). The picture painted in modern revelation is one of vast portions of the spirit world, "the hosts of the dead, both small and great" (v. 11) abuzz with increasing excitement over and conversation about the physical death, atoning sacrifice, and spirit appearance of the great Messiah.

They were not disappointed! He did come. As the revelation states,

> While this vast multitude waited and conversed, rejoicing in the hour of their deliverance from the chains of death, the Son of God appeared, declaring liberty to the captives who had been faithful;
>
> And there he preached to them the everlasting gospel, the doctrine of the resurrection and the redemption of mankind from the fall, and from individual sins on conditions of repentance. (D&C 138:18–19)

Surely, in the long history of our Heavenly Father's great plan of happiness, few events have witnessed as tremendous an outpouring of rejoicing and exultation as the Savior's appearance to the righteous dead in the world of spirits.

This leads us to our fourth point of comparison between the environment at Golgotha and the environment of the spirit world. The atmosphere at Golgotha was infused and suffused with brutality, coarseness, and wickedness. Crucifixion itself was a brutal and bloody business from start to finish. The Jewish and Roman leaders who condemned Jesus to death, as well as the soldiers who carried out the sentence of execution, were brutal and bloody men. Moreover, the chief Apostle, Peter, had testified to the men of Judea that Jesus was crucified and slain by "wicked hands" (Acts 2:23).

Contrast the foregoing with the environment of the spirit world. The latter was filled with righteousness. Those who waited with joyful anticipation for our Lord's advent were some of the best, most righteous souls that God the Father had created and caused to be placed on this earth. They were the noble and great ones of our premortal existence.

Among the great and mighty ones who were assembled in this vast congregation of the righteous were Father Adam, the Ancient of Days and father of all,

And our glorious Mother Eve, with many of her faithful daughters who had lived through the ages and worshiped the true and living God.

Abel, the first martyr, was there, and his brother Seth, one of the mighty ones, who was in the express image of his father, Adam.

Noah, who gave warning of the flood; Shem, the great high priest; Abraham, the father of the faithful; Isaac, Jacob, and Moses, the great law-giver of Israel. (D&C 138:38–41)

Moreover, there were Isaiah, Ezekiel, Daniel, Elias, and Malachi (see vv. 42–46). "All these and many more, even the prophets who dwelt among the Nephites and testified of the coming of the Son of God, mingled in the vast assembly and waited for their deliverance" (v. 49).

What an amazing assembly this was. And what a glorious atmosphere prevailed. It must have been even more emotionally powerful than described in scripture, as our first parents, Adam and Eve, welcomed Jesus Christ into their midst: the very Son of God but also one of their very own posterity, a member of *their* family, who had rescued and ransomed all the other members of their family—the entire human race.

Jesus' appearance in the spirit world was the embodiment of freedom and redemption, and all the righteous spirits knew it. "For [all] the dead had looked upon the long absence of their spirits from their bodies as a bondage" (D&C 138:50). We usually speak of a portion of the spirit world as "spirit prison," the place where the wicked spirits, as well as those yet unbaptized, dwell apart from the righteous spirits who are in paradise. And yet the truth is that the whole of the spirit world was a prison to all who resided there.

Even though the spirits of the righteous will be happy in paradise, they will not be—cannot be—truly and completely happy while a part of them is lying in the grave. In the language of the revelations of the Restoration, the spirit and the body are the soul of man. When inseparably connected, the spirit and the physical body can receive a fulness of joy. When separated, they cannot receive a fulness of joy (D&C 88:15; 93:33; 138:17). Without their physical bodies, the spirits of all men and women "are in prison," said President Brigham Young.[6]

Elder Melvin J. Ballard gave this explanation:

> I grant you that the righteous dead will be at peace, but I tell you that when we go out of this life, leave this body, we will desire to do many things that we cannot do at all without the body. We will be seriously handicapped, and we will long for the body; we then will pray for the early reunion with our bodies. . . .
>
> . . . We are sentencing ourselves to long periods of bondage, separating our spirits from our bodies, or we are shortening that period, according to the way in which we overcome and master ourselves [in mortality].[7]

Thus, through his atoning sacrifice and subsequent resurrection, Jesus Christ opened the prison doors to the righteous as well as the wicked. He fulfilled Isaiah's messianic prophecy, spoken more than seven hundred years earlier and which he quoted during his mortal ministry: "The Lord hath anointed me to preach good tidings unto the meek; he hath sent me to bind up the brokenhearted, to proclaim liberty to the captives, and the opening of the prison to them that are bound" (Isaiah 61:1; see also Luke 4:16–20).

WHAT THE SAVIOR DID

This leads us then to discuss the second focal point of the Savior's spirit-world ministry—what he did and did *not* do while he was there. It is important to understand that after Jesus died, he did not immediately enter the physical presence of his father, our Father in Heaven. Perhaps a misunderstanding on this point arises from the language of Alma, who stated, "The spirits of all men, as soon as they are departed from this mortal body, yea, the spirits of all men, whether they be good or evil, are taken home to that God who gave them life" (Alma 40:11). Several of the early apostles and prophets of this present dispensation have helped us to understand Alma's language.[8] Perhaps the clearest interpretation of Alma's use of the phrase "taken home to that God who gave them life" was offered by President George Q. Cannon, counselor in the First Presidency for many years.

> Alma, when he says that "the spirits of all men, as soon as they are departed from this mortal body, . . . are taken home to that God who gave them life," has the idea, doubtless, in his mind that our God is omnipresent—not in His own personality but through His minister, the Holy Spirit.

President George Q. Cannon
(© Intellectual Reserve, Inc.)

He does not intend to convey the idea that they are immediately ushered into the personal presence of God. He evidently uses that phrase in a qualified sense. Solomon . . . makes a similar statement: "Then shall the dust return to the earth as it was: and the spirit shall return unto God who gave it." (Ecclesiastes 12:7.) The same idea is frequently expressed by the Latter-day Saints. In referring to a departed one it is often said that he has gone back to God, or he has gone "home to that God who gave him life." Yet it would not be contended that the person who said this meant that the departed one had gone where God, the Father Himself is, in the sense in which the Savior meant when He spake to Mary.⁹

When Jesus arrived in the spirit world, he commenced a unique work, something that had never been done before. President Brigham Young declared, "Jesus was the first man that ever went to preach to the spirits in prison, holding the keys of the Gospel of salvation to them. Those keys were delivered to him in the day and hour that he went into the spirit world, and with them he opened the door of salvation to the spirits in prison."[10]

The Savior's visit to the spirit world, and the commencement of his unique work among the dead, involved as much delegation of authority as did his ministry in mortality. President Joseph F. Smith saw for himself that Jesus Christ confined his visit to paradise and that, as holder of the keys of the work for the dead, he commissioned and organized the faithful spirits in paradise to visit the other spirits of the unbaptized, unrighteous, ungodly, unrepentant, disobedient, rebellious, and ignorant in order to proclaim liberty to them by teaching the gospel of Jesus Christ. President Smith stated:

I perceived that the Lord went not in person among the wicked and disobedient who had rejected the truth, to teach them;

But behold, from among the righteous, he organized his forces and appointed messengers, clothed with power and authority, and commissioned them to go forth and carry the light of the gospel to them that were in darkness, even to all the spirits of men; and thus was the gospel preached to the dead. (D&C 138:29–30)

Jesus did not go in person to the wicked in the spirit world, nor to any who were unbaptized, which is the great determining factor that differentiates those in paradise from those in spirit prison.[11] Jesus did not, would not, reenter the environment from which he had just come in mortality (which is one reason I began by comparing the environments of Golgotha and paradise.) Jesus would no longer stand among the wicked and rebellious. Rather, he organized a mission.

All of the ancients we have already mentioned by name, beginning with Adam and Eve, formed part of the missionary force organized to teach the gospel to those in spirit prison. They were delegated keys of power and authority to do so by the Savior. Just as none in mortality are sanctioned to go forth to preach the gospel or build up the Church without authorization (D&C 42:11), so none in the spirit world were sent forth without being given authority.

Such delegation by the Lord Jesus Christ implies the continuing operation of the priesthood in the world of spirits. "As in earth, so in the spirit world," declared Elder Parley P. Pratt. "No person can enter into the privileges of the Gospel, until the keys are turned, and the Gospel opened by those in authority."[12] Of the authorized ministers in the spirit world, President Joseph F. Smith further said, "They are there, having carried with them from here the holy Priesthood that they received under authority, and which was conferred upon them in the flesh."[13] President Brigham Young observed that "when a person passes behind the vail [sic], he can . . . officiate in the spirit-world;

but when he is resurrected he officiates as a resurrected being, and not as a mortal being."[14]

The Savior's work among the righteous dead in the spirit world, and his act of delegating authority to them so they could help others there, enlarges our picture of the operation of the priesthood in time and eternity. Truly, the priesthood is eternal. Its existence spans premortality, mortality, and the postmortal world. The Prophet Joseph Smith declared, "The Priesthood is an everlasting principle, and existed with God from eternity, and will to eternity, without beginning of days or end of years."[15] Moreover, modern prophets have declared that righteous men did indeed hold the priesthood in our *premortal* existence. President Joseph Fielding Smith presents us with this insightful declaration: "With regard to the holding of the priesthood in the preexistence, I will say that there was an organization there just as well as an organization here, and men there held authority. Men chosen to positions of trust in the spirit world held the priesthood."[16] The foregoing is consistent with President Joseph F. Smith's panoramic vision and perspective found in Doctrine and Covenants 138, which also spanned premortality and the postmortal spirit world. Speaking of the missionaries and ministers of the gospel in the spirit world, he said: "I observed that they were also among the noble and great ones who were chosen in the beginning to be rulers in the Church of God. Even before they were born, they, with many others, received their first lessons in the world of spirits and were prepared to come forth in the due time of the Lord to labor in his vineyard for the salvation of the souls of men" (D&C 138:55–56). President Joseph F. Smith also saw that the missionary work begun in the spirit world at the time Jesus inaugurated his spirit-prison mission continues in our own day by "the faithful elders of this dispensation" who have passed on (D&C 138:57).

Memories of my own father come flooding back to my mind when I read this portion of President Smith's vision. My father was a member of the Seventy and a stake missionary at the time he passed away, a real force for missionary work in the area where we lived. Even at a young age, I could tell he felt genuine passion for the work and for his quorum. My father's regular Sunday assignment was teaching a special Gospel Doctrine class to inmates at the nearby federal prison. I know he cherished that opportunity. I have thought since, and I believe it so, that he is again engaged in teaching prisoners, but prisoners of a different kind. Missionary work carries on in the postmortal spirit world.

Priesthood holders are not the only ones involved in this work among the dead. President Joseph F. Smith offered this truly profound and significant insight about sisters involved in the work of salvation in the spirit world:

Now, among all these millions of spirits that have lived on the earth and have passed away, from generation to

generation, since the be-
ginning of the world,
without the knowledge of
the gospel—among them
you may count that at least
one-half are women. Who
is going to preach the gospel to the women? Who
is going to carry the testimony of Jesus Christ to the
hearts of the women who
have passed away without
a knowledge of the gospel?

President Joseph F. Smith
(Courtesy of Wikimedia.)

Well, to my mind, it is a simple thing. These good sisters
who have been set apart, ordained to the work, called to
it, authorized by the authority of the holy Priesthood to
minister for their sex, in the House of God for the living and for the dead, will be fully authorized and em-
powered to preach the gospel and minister to the women
while the elders and prophets are preaching it to the men.
The things we experience here are typical of the things
of God and the life beyond us. There is a great similarity
between God's purposes as manifested here and his purposes as carried out in his presence and kingdom. Those

who are authorized to preach the gospel here and are appointed here to do that work will not be idle after they have passed away, but will continue to exercise the rights that they obtained here under the Priesthood of the Son of God to minister for the salvation of those who have died without a knowledge of the truth.[17]

Just as sisters in this life are called and authorized to preach the gospel on the earth, often working among other women, so sisters in the next life are called and authorized to be messengers of the Lord's gospel, ministering specifically among women. It will be remembered that President Smith made it a point of stating explicitly in his vision of the spirit world that he saw "our glorious Mother Eve, with many of her faithful daughters who had lived through the ages and worshiped the true and living God" (D&C 138:39). It is to be assumed that these were part of the Savior's "forces and appointed messengers, clothed with power and authority, and commissioned . . . to go forth and carry the light of the gospel to them that were in darkness" (D&C 138:30).

CONCLUSION

Truly, the gospel is for all of our Heavenly Father's children—"black and white, bond and free, male and female; and he remembereth the heathen; and all are alike unto God" (2 Nephi 26:33). In no place or way do we see with greater clarity the fulfillment of this scripture than in the Savior's continuing ministry to the spirit world. The chief Apostle in the meridian dispensation, Peter, confirmed Nephi's statement about God's all-inclusive love and fairness when he explained how the Atonement applies to both the living and the dead and why Jesus went to the spirit world after his mortal mission was finished: "For Christ also hath once suffered for sins, the just for the unjust, that he might bring us to God, being put to death in the flesh, but quickened by the Spirit: by which also he went and preached unto the spirits in prison. . . . For for this cause was the gospel preached also to them that are dead, that they might be judged according to men in the flesh, but live according to God in the spirit" (1 Peter 3:18–19; 4:6).

These verses are quite remarkable. Many in the Christian community cannot fully explain them. But as Latter-day Saints, we can imagine quite easily what powerful visions of the spirit world Peter was privileged to see that enabled him to teach this doctrine so succinctly and with such power. His experience must have been akin to Joseph F. Smith's manifestation as recorded in Doctrine and Covenants 138.

Before the coming of Jesus to the world of spirits, those spirits could not be judged according to men in the flesh while living according to God in the spirit, because the gospel had not ever been preached to the dead. The great gulf that existed between paradise and spirit prison had not been bridged. Baptisms for the dead had not been performed. "Not until Christ had organized his missionary forces in the world of spirits do we find references to the Saints practicing the ordinance of baptism for the dead (1 Cor. 15:29)."[18] Jesus' visit to the spirit world changed the universe forever. Those "dead who had been confined in darkness *not knowing their fate*" could be set free.[19]

With the great gulf in the spirit world finally bridged after thousands of years of waiting on the part of all those who had died from Adam to Christ, Jesus was prepared to fulfill the next phase of the glorious and infinite Atonement—his Resurrection. But Jesus Christ's ministry to the spirit world is by itself a powerful testimony of God's perfect love and concern for all his children.

I am grateful for this profound knowledge of the spirit world, communicated to us through modern prophets. This full understanding can be found nowhere else except in The Church of Jesus Christ of Latter-day Saints. Because of this knowledge, death need not hold any fear for disciples of Jesus Christ. For the righteous, those who strive to live the gospel of faith, repentance, baptism, and the gift of the Holy Ghost, the spirit world will be a place of peace, rest, and security. President George Q. Cannon gave us the assurance that "Satan is bound as soon as the faithful spirit leaves this tabernacle of clay and goes to the other side of the veil. That spirit is emancipated from the power and thralldom and attacks of Satan. Satan can only afflict such in this life."[20]

Furthermore, those that pass into the spirit world will find it to be a place of great reunion. Again, President Cannon stated, "How delightful it is to contemplate the departure of those who have been faithful, as far as their knowledge permitted, to the truth which God has revealed! There is no sting nor gloom nor inconsolable sorrow about the departure of such persons. Holy angels are around their bedside to administer unto them. The Spirit of God rests down upon them, and His messengers are near them to introduce them to those who are on the other side of the veil."[21]

President Joseph F. Smith added this thought: "What is more desirable than that we should meet with our fathers and our mothers, with our brethren and our sisters, with our wives and our children, with our beloved associates and kindred in the spirit world, knowing each other, identifying each other . . . by the associations that familiarize each to the other in mortal life? What do you want better than that?"[22]

Last, but not least, the spirit world will be a place of great learning to baptized disciples of Jesus Christ. Elder Orson Pratt of the Quorum of the Twelve spoke powerfully of the increased capacities of spirits in paradise to learn, grow intellectually, and increase in knowledge exponentially:

When I speak of the future state of man, and the situation of our spirits between death and the resurrection, I long for the experience and knowledge to be gained in that state, as well as this. We shall learn many more things there; we need not suppose our five senses connect us with all the things of heaven, and earth, and eternity, and space; we need not think that we are conversant with all the elements of nature, through the medium of the senses God has given us here. Suppose He should give us a sixth sense, a seventh, an eighth, a ninth, or a fiftieth. All these different senses would convey to us new ideas, as much so as the senses of tasting, smelling, or seeing communicate different ideas from that of hearing.[23]

In sum, President Joseph F. Smith said of paradise, it is a place where the righteous can "expand in wisdom, where they have respite from all their troubles, and where care and sorrow [will] not annoy."[24] Paradise will be a place where our spirit bodies will be free to think and act with renewed capacity, vigor, and enthusiasm that will prepare us for eternal life, which is made possible by the Atonement of Jesus Christ.

NOTES

1. Hugh Nibley, *The Prophetic Book of Mormon* (Salt Lake City: Deseret Book, 1989), 428.

2. Hyrum L. Andrus, *God, Man, and the Universe* (Salt Lake City: Bookcraft, 1973), 452.

3. James E. Talmage, *Jesus the Christ* (Salt Lake City: Deseret Book, 1984), 620–21.

4. *Teachings of Presidents of the Church: Brigham Young* (Salt Lake City: The

Church of Jesus Christ of Latter-day Saints, 1997), 279.

5. Parley P. Pratt, *Key to the Science of Theology* (London: Latter-day Saints' Book Depot, 1855), 80.

6. Brigham Young, in *Journal of Discourses* (London: Latter-day Saints' Book Depot, 1854–86), 3:95.

7. Melvin J. Ballard, "The Three Degrees of Glory," in *Sermons and Missionary Services of Melvin J. Ballard*, ed. Bryant S. Hinckley (Salt Lake City: Deseret Book, 1949), 240–42.

8. See, for example, Brigham Young, in *Journal of Discourses*, 3:368; and Orson Pratt, in *Journal of Discourses*, 16:332–33.

9. *Gospel Truth: Discourses and Writings of President George Q. Cannon*, ed. Jerreld L. Newquist (Salt Lake City: Deseret Book, 1957), 57–58.

10. *Teachings of Presidents of the Church: Brigham Young*, 280.

11. Joseph Fielding Smith, *Doctrines of Salvation*, comp. Bruce R. McConkie (Salt Lake City: Bookcraft, 1954–56), 2:230.

12. Parley P. Pratt, in *Journal of Discourses*, 1:11.

13. Joseph F. Smith, *Gospel Doctrine* (Salt Lake City: Deseret Book, 1986), 471.

14. Brigham Young, in *Journal of Discourses*, 9:88–89.

15. Joseph Smith, in *Journal of Discourses*, 6:237.

16. Joseph Fielding Smith, in Conference Report, October 1966, 84.

17. Smith, *Gospel Doctrine*, 461.

18. Robert L. Millet and Joseph Fielding McConkie, *The Life Beyond* (Salt Lake City: Deseret Book, 1986), 51.

19. Joseph Fielding Smith, *Answers to Gospel Questions* (Salt Lake City: Deseret Book, 1958), 2:81.

20. *Gospel Truth*, 61.

21. *Gospel Truth*, 61.

22. Joseph F. Smith, "The Resurrection," *Liahona: The Elders' Journal*, August 8, 1908, 178.

23. Orson Pratt, in *Journal of Discourses*, 2:247.

24. Smith, *Gospel Doctrine*, 448.

The doctrine of salvation for the dead . . . provides the perfect balance between justice and mercy. Without that balance—without that plan—God could neither be all loving and merciful nor perfectly fair and just.

(Courtesy of Toby Hudson.)

A Perfect Balance of Justice and Mercy

Brent L. Top

WHILE PRESIDING OVER the Illinois Peoria Mission, my wife and I had the privilege of taking every group of departing missionaries on their last day in the mission field to the Nauvoo Temple for an endowment session. It became my practice to greet each elder and sister as they entered the celestial room with a big hug and a whispered expression of my love and appreciation for their service and commitment. I had been the beneficiary of just such a hug and tender expressions by Elder Dieter F. Uchtdorf, then a member of the Quorum of the Twelve Apostles, at an area mission presidents' seminar at the first of our mission. It was a critical turning

Brent L. Top is a professor of Church history and doctrine at Brigham Young University. He presided over the Illinois Peoria Mission from 2004 to 2007.

point of our mission—a time when I felt totally overwhelmed and inadequate. Elder Uchtdorf's expression of love at that moment was a monumentally transforming event for me, and I wanted my missionaries to feel something akin to what I felt from him. I must admit, however, that it was easier to express those sentiments to some missionaries than it was to others. (Perhaps Elder Uchtdorf had the same feelings about me!)

One elder in particular had given me more than his share of grief. In fact, many of the gray hairs that came after I was called as mission president can be attributed to him. He seemed to be in trouble all the time. On more than one occasion, I told him that I was going to send him home. Yet he would always promise me that he would try harder. His renewed commitment seldom lasted very long, however. And the cycle of rebuke, repentance, recommitment, and relapse would start all over again. Perhaps it would have been easier to have just sent him home. Yet I could see some of me in him, and I wanted him to succeed. I wanted him to return with honor. He wasn't an all-star, but now he had made it. He completed his mission and accompanied us to the temple before he flew home.

As he came into the celestial room, I greeted him with the customary "I love you." Tears streamed down his face. "Thank you for extending me mercy," he whispered as his whole body shook with weeping. It was a tender moment, and both of us shed many tears of

Christ's mercy is the very essence of the message of Easter.
(James Tissot, *The Return of the Prodigal Son*, © Intellectual Reserve, Inc.)

gratitude. Almost as if the veil parted, I sensed a coming day when I would embrace the Savior and with tears of thanksgiving and love say, "Thank you for extending me mercy."

It is of the Savior's mercy that I wish to speak. His mercy is the very essence of the message of Easter, and I wish to add my personal testimony and expression of gratitude for his mercy that has been extended to me individually and for his "plan of mercy" that is available to all people. I echo the words of the Book of Mormon prophet Jacob: "O how great the goodness of our God, who prepareth a way for our escape from the grasp of this awful monster; yea, that monster, death and hell, which I call the death of the body, and also the death of the spirit" (2 Nephi 9:10). It is easy, especially at Easter time, to celebrate God's infinite goodness and his tender mercy. Not often, however, do we hear declarations or observe celebrations of his perfect justice. Yet each is an integral by-product of the Atonement of Jesus Christ. In fact, the gospel of Jesus Christ—what the scriptures call "the merciful plan of the great Creator" (2 Nephi 9:6), the "plan of redemption" (Alma 34:16), "the great plan of the Eternal God" (Alma 34:9), "the plan of restoration" (Alma 41:2), "the great plan of happiness" (Alma 42:8), and "the plan of mercy" (Alma 42:15)—is the perfect balance between God's justice *and* his mercy. The Book of Mormon prophet Alma explained, "And now, the plan of mercy could not be brought about except an atonement should be made; therefore God himself atoneth for the sins of the world, to bring about the plan of mercy, to appease the demands of justice, that God might be a perfect, just God, and a merciful God also" (Alma 42:15).

How can this be? How can the Lord be both merciful and just? How can he mercifully save some individuals who don't "deserve" or "merit" being saved (see Alma 22:14) and yet, as some Christians teach, damn those who lack the knowledge of Jesus in this life and thus the opportunity to be saved? How can the Perfect One be perfectly loving and longsuffering, perfectly kind and caring, perfectly merciful and magnanimous, and yet perfectly and uncompromisingly earnest when he says the following?

> He that believeth and is baptized shall be saved; but he that believeth not shall be damned. (Mark 16:16)

> Except a man be born of water and of the Spirit, he cannot enter into the kingdom of God. (John 3:5)

> And by him all that believe are justified from all things. (Acts 13:39)

> If thou shalt confess with thy mouth the Lord Jesus, and shalt believe in thine heart that God hath raised him from the dead, thou shalt be saved. (Romans 10:9)

There are numerous scriptural statements, not just in the Bible but throughout all the standard works, that teach and testify of the uncompromising conditions and commandments linked to salvation. King Benjamin taught that salvation comes to none "except it be through repentance and faith on the Lord Jesus Christ" (Mosiah 3:12) and that mercy has no claim on the unbelieving and unrepentant (see Mosiah 2:38–39). Similarly, Alma taught that "whosoever repenteth shall find mercy; and he that findeth mercy and endureth to the end . . . shall be saved" (Alma 32:13). In this dispensation, the Lord has further declared:

And we know that all men must repent and believe on the name of Jesus Christ, and worship the Father in his name, and endure in faith on his name to the end, or they cannot be saved in the kingdom of God. (D&C 20:29)

Yea, repent and be baptized, every one of you, for a remission of your sins; yea, be baptized even by water, and then cometh the baptism of fire and of the Holy Ghost.

Behold, verily, verily, I say unto you, this is my gospel; and remember that they shall have faith in me or they can in nowise be saved. (D&C 33:11–12)

Thus saith the Lord; for I am God, and have sent mine Only Begotten Son into the world for the redemption of the world, and have decreed that he that receiveth him shall be saved, and he that receiveth him not shall be damned. (D&C 49:5)

And he that believeth and is baptized shall be saved, and he that believeth not shall be damned. (D&C 68:9; see also D&C 112:29)

Many similar passages could be cited, but these excerpts are sufficient to show that God's word is clear and unequivocal regarding what he requires of his children for eternal salvation. There doesn't appear to be much "wiggle room." And if there were "wiggle room," how would that affect the perfect justice of God? Does the Lord say one thing and then do something different—changing the rules in the middle of the game, or changing the score after the game? The answer seems to be a clear-cut no. A perfectly just God will change neither the rules of the game nor the final score, so to speak. To do so would not be just. But that fact of life—the eternal law of justice, in and of itself—also raises difficult questions and real-life dilemmas. Let me illustrate this concept from a relatively recent best-selling book and the spirited reactions to it that followed (and that continue today).

Rob Bell was the founding pastor of Mars Hill Bible Church in Grandville, Michigan, which became one of the fastest-growing congregations in the United States. His sermons, writings, and videos applying gospel teachings to real-life needs made him one of the most visible, influential, and sought-after religious voices in the country. In 2011, *Time* magazine named him one of the "100 Most Influential People in the World." His book *Love Wins* became a *New York Times* best seller, and it became as controversial as it was popular. The very first chapter begins with these challenging examples and even more challenging questions:

> Several years ago we had an art show at our church. I had been giving a series of teachings on peacemaking, and we invited artists to display their paintings, poems, and sculptures that reflected their understanding of what it means to be a peacemaker. One woman included in her work a quote from Mahatma Gandhi, which a number of people found quite compelling.
>
> But not everyone.
>
> Someone attached a piece of paper to it.
>
> On the piece of paper was written: "Reality check: He's in hell."
>
> Really?
>
> Gandhi's in hell?

He is?

We have confirmation of this?

Somebody knows this?

Without a doubt?

And that somebody decided to take on the responsibility of letting the rest of us know?

Of all the billions of people who have ever lived, will only a select number "make it to a better place" and every single other person suffer in torment and punishment forever? Is this acceptable to God? Has God created millions of people over tens of thousands of years who are going to spend eternity in anguish? Can God do this, or even allow this, and still claim to be a loving God?

Does God punish people for thousands of years with infinite, eternal torment for things they did in their few finite years of life?

This doesn't just raise disturbing questions about God; it raises questions about the beliefs themselves.

Why them?

Why you?

Why me?

If there are only a select few who go to heaven, which is more terrifying to fathom: the billions who burn forever

or the few who escape this fate? How does a person end
up being one of the few?

Chance?

Luck?

Random selection?

Being born in the right place, family, or country?

Having a youth pastor who "relates better to the kids"?

What kind of faith is that?

Or, more important: What kind of God is that?[1]

Bell provides another example that leads to more questions and challenging issues.

Several years ago I heard a woman tell about the funeral
of her daughter's friend, a high-school student who was
killed in a car accident. Her daughter was asked by a
Christian if the young man who had died was a Christian.
She said that he told people he was an atheist. This person
then said to her, "So there's no hope then."

No hope?

Is that the Christian message?

"No hope"?

Is that what Jesus offers the world?[2]

Interestingly, Pastor Bell raises the issue of the age of accountability. Was the young man actually accountable for the decisions he made (or did not make) at such a young age? Could he have changed his mind or his life with a little more time and maturity? What could he have done differently to not be in the "no hope" status? The author continues:

> Would he have had to perform a specific rite or ritual?
>
> Or take a class?
>
> Or be baptized?
>
> Or join a church?
>
> Or have something happen somewhere in his heart?
>
> Some believe he would have had to say a specific prayer. Christians don't agree on exactly what this prayer is, but for many the essential idea is that the only way to get into heaven is to pray at some point in your life, asking God to forgive you and telling God that you accept Jesus, you believe Jesus died on the cross to pay the price for your sins, and you want to go to heaven when you die. Some call this "accepting Christ," others call it the "sinner's prayer," and still others call it "getting saved," being "born again," or being "converted."
>
> That, of course, raises more questions. What about people who have said some form of "the prayer" at some

point in their life, but it means nothing to them today?
. . .

What about people who have never said the prayer and
don't claim to be Christians, but live a more Christlike
life than some Christians? . . .

Which leads to a far more disturbing question. So is
it true that the kind of person you are doesn't ultimately
matter, as long as you've said or prayed or believed the
right things?[3]

This book has created a firestorm of reaction. Some applauded
the fact that the author was willing to ask tough questions and chal-
lenge traditional beliefs. Others—many, many others—passionately
renounced his suppositions and declared his teachings as unbiblical
at best and heretical at worst. Some even characterized him as "worse
than the infidel" and condemned him to the very hell he was challenging. Pastor Bell did not create the theological controversy, nor
did his words settle the issue. He once again raised an important
question, and the question still remains—the same question that was
asked in the early days of Christ's church in the meridian of time
and is asked today by both scholars and seekers: "What is the fate
of those who die never hearing of the gospel of Jesus Christ?" In the
book *What About Those Who Have Never Heard?* Christian theolo-
gian John Sanders wrote:

Are all the "heathen" lost? Is there an opportunity for those who have never heard of Jesus to be saved?

These questions raise one of the most perplexing, provocative and perennial issues facing Christians. It has been considered by philosophers and farmers, Christians and non-Christians. In societies where Christianity has had strong influence, just about everyone has either asked or been asked about the final destiny of those dying without knowledge of the only Savior, Jesus Christ. Far and away, this is the most asked apologetic question on U.S. college campuses.[4]

Sanders provided a poignant insight into the very personal nature of this issue. He explained that he and his wife adopted three children from India. One of those children later asked if there was any hope for the salvation of her birth parents since they probably had never even heard about Jesus. Those Indian birth parents are but two of the vast majority of the human family who have ever lived or will yet live on this planet who have never known the Savior or heard his gospel taught. He then explained that as we have more and more contact with people from different countries, cultures, and religious traditions, we will more frequently encounter questions concerning the ultimate destiny of friends and family who have never heard of the "good news" of Christ's gospel. "What may be said," Sanders asked, "about the destiny of countless billions who have lived and died apart from any understanding of the divine grace manifested in Jesus?"[5]

Much has been written through the years by Christian scholars in response to these questions. It is not my purpose in this setting—nor am I qualified—to adequately review the various philosophical schools of thought or theological explanations. Professor Robert L. Millet has done a wonderful job in doing just that in an article entitled "The Soteriological Problem of Evil."[6] What I do know, however, is that each explanation, at least to my understanding, is inadequate in maintaining the delicate balance between God's justice and his mercy. At one end of the philosophical continuum is pluralism (or universalism) and at the other end is exclusivism. A pluralist would advocate for a universal salvation—that God is working his will in all the world, gradually lifting and transforming them to a condition where all will eventually be saved in God's heaven, regardless of race, religion, culture, or tradition. We can certainly see, in such a view, God's infinite mercy. However, this doesn't seem to account for much of God's justice. On the other hand, an exclusivist would declare that people are saved only if they accept the Lord Jesus Christ *in this life*. Sanders summarized the exclusivist position: "Our destinies are sealed at death and no opportunity for salvation exists after that."[7] Such a view certainly emphasizes that God really means it when he talks about the necessity of accepting Christ and meeting the conditions of salvation established in scripture. That is justice. However, there doesn't seem to be any mercy—any exceptions or provisions for those who never had the opportunity to hear the gospel and embrace it.

Exclusivism, in varying forms, was a prevalent notion in Joseph Smith's religious milieu. No wonder he was surprised when, in his vision of the celestial kingdom, he saw his deceased brother Alvin in that exalted condition, "seeing that he had departed this life before the Lord had set his hand to gather Israel the second time, and had not been baptized for the remission of sins" (D&C 137:6). Reverend Benjamin Stockton, who was minister of the Presbyterian church that Lucy Mack Smith attended and who conducted Alvin's funeral, declared that Alvin was likely in hell because he died without a proper Christian baptism and had not been a regular church attender.[8] No doubt this statement had a powerful impact on young Joseph and his family—an impact that is reflected in the Prophet's teachings even two decades later. "The idea that some men form of the justice, judgment, and mercy of God, is too foolish for an intelligent man to think of," Joseph wrote in an editorial in the *Times and Seasons* in 1842. "For instance, it is common for many of our orthodox preachers to suppose that if a man is not what they call converted, if he dies in that state he must remain eternally in hell without any hope. Infinite years in torment must he spend, and never, never, never have an end; and yet this eternal misery is made frequently to rest upon the merest casualty."[9] On another occasion, the Prophet declared: "One dies and is buried, having never heard the Gospel of reconciliation; to the other the message of salvation is sent, he hears and embraces it, and is made the heir of eternal life. Shall the one become the partaker of glory and the other be consigned to hopeless perdition? Is there no chance for his escape? Sectarianism answers 'none.' Such an idea is worse than atheism."[10]

With the remarkable vision of the celestial kingdom that Joseph Smith received in the Kirtland Temple on January 21, 1836, the Lord revealed to the Prophet that "all who have died without a knowledge of this gospel, who would have received it if they had been permitted to tarry, shall be heirs of the celestial kingdom of God; also all that shall die henceforth without a knowledge of it, who would have received it with all their hearts, shall be heirs of that kingdom" (D&C 137:7–8). Although at the time the Prophet may not have fully understood all the details regarding the redemption of the dead, it was abundantly clear that for his brother Alvin and the billions of God's children who lived and died without knowledge of the gospel, the Lord's arms of saving mercy are outstretched—to all peoples of the earth in all dispensations of time (see Alma 5:33). Neither the exclusivists nor the universalists are right. The plan of salvation, revealed in this dispensation through the Prophet Joseph Smith, with its unique provisions for those who never had an opportunity to come unto Christ, cut a new path between the two. The very next phrase in the scriptural account reveals the divine balance between mercy and justice. "For I, the Lord, will judge all men according to their works, according to the desire of their hearts" (D&C 137:9). With this new revelation, the Apostle Peter's ancient teachings become clearer.

> For Christ also hath once suffered for sins, the just for the unjust, that he might bring us to God, being put to death in the flesh, but quickened by the Spirit:
>
> By which also he went and preached unto the spirits in prison. (1 Peter 3:18–19)

> For this cause was the gospel preached also to them that are dead, *that they might be judged according to men in the flesh, but live according to God in the spirit.* (1 Peter 4:6; emphasis added)

The justice of God requires that all be "judged according to men in the flesh"—meaning that the standard or law by which men can receive salvation is the same for all. There are no sliding scales, grades on the curve, bargain days, or backroom deals. That is justice. Yet humankind will be judged "according to the desire of their hearts" and by whether they "live according to God in the spirit"—meaning that all will be given a full and fair opportunity, in this life or the next, to hear the gospel, understand its principles, feel the Spirit bear witness of its truth, and choose either to have faith in Christ and submit to his gospel or to reject it. That is mercy. The doctrine of salvation for the dead as revealed to the Prophet Joseph Smith in the last days provides the perfect balance between justice and mercy. Without that balance—without that plan—God could neither be all loving and merciful nor perfectly fair and just.

In his remarkable vision of the redemption of the dead, President Joseph F. Smith learned that the disembodied Savior of the world, in his infinite love and mercy for mankind, "organized his forces and appointed messengers [in the postmortal spirit world], clothed with power and authority, and commissioned them to go forth and carry the light of the gospel to them that were in darkness, *even to all the spirits of men*; and thus was the gospel preached to the dead" (D&C 138:30; emphasis added). Those who died without an opportunity as well as those who had been taught, yet rejected the truth and died in their sins, will once again be taught and given every chance to repent of their sins and come unto the Lord (see v. 32). God's mercy is manifest in *who* is taught in the spirit world. His justice is manifest in *what* is taught there.

> These were taught *faith* in God, *repentance* from sin, vicarious *baptism* for the remission of sins, the *gift of the Holy Ghost* by the laying on of hands,
>
> And *all other principles of the gospel* that were necessary for them to know in order to qualify themselves *that they might be judged according to men in the flesh, but live according to God in the spirit.* (vv. 33–34; emphasis added)

At this Easter season we rejoice in and testify of the reality of Christ's Resurrection—the culmination of his infinite Atonement. Because of that, we can also rightly rejoice in the plan of salvation— the perfect balance between justice and mercy—that is made available to all mankind. As Alma declared:

> Mercy claimeth the penitent, and mercy cometh because of the atonement; and the atonement bringeth to pass the resurrection of the dead; and the resurrection of the dead bringeth back men into the presence of God; and thus they are restored into his presence, to be judged according to their works, according to the law and justice.
>
> For behold, justice exerciseth all his demands, and also mercy claimeth all which is her own; and thus, none but the truly penitent are saved. (Alma 42:23–24)

I return, in closing, to the Nauvoo Temple and the missionary who, through his tears, exclaimed, "Thank you for extending me mercy." On this Easter—and every day—I see myself in him. In the coming day, I hope it will be me who is "clasped in the arms of Jesus" (Mormon 5:11), tearfully and with eternal gratitude saying, "Thank you for extending me mercy." But my gratitude will extend beyond just my own salvation. I will further declare, "Thank you for extending mercy to my family—those of my earthly family and

the billions constituting that portion of humanity who never knew
of the Savior's mercy in mortality. Thank you for the plan of salvation—the plan of mercy—that justly and mercifully reaches out to
all my brothers and sisters." I gratefully add my testimony to that
of the Prophet Joseph Smith. "All are within the reach of pardon-
ing mercy," he taught in the October 1841 general conference in
Nauvoo. "This doctrine appears glorious, inasmuch as it exhibits the
greatness of divine compassion and benevolence in the extent of the
plan of human salvation . . . [and] is well calculated to enlarge the
understanding, and sustain the soul under troubles, difficulties and
distresses."[11]

Jesus is risen. He lives. His mercy is more than I can compre-
hend. My gratitude and love are more than I can adequately express.
My heart exclaims with Jacob, "O how great the goodness of our
God" (2 Nephi 9:10)!

NOTES

1. Rob Bell, *Love Wins* (New York: Harper One, 2011), 1–3.
2. Bell, *Love Wins*, 3.
3. Bell, *Love Wins*, 5–6.
4. Gabriel Fackre, Ronald H. Nash, and John Sanders, *What About Those Who Have Never Heard? Three Views on the Destiny of the Unevangelized* (Downers Grove, IL: InterVarsity, 1995), 7.
5. Fackre, Nash, and Sanders, *What About Those Who Have Never Heard?*, 9.
6. Robert L. Millet, "The Soteriological Problem of Evil," *Religious Educator* 2, no. 2 (2001): 73–82. See also David L. Paulsen, Kendel J. Christensen, and Martin Pulido, "Redeeming the Dead: Tender Mercies, Turning of

Hearts, and Restoration of Authority," *Journal of the Book of Mormon and Other Restoration Scripture* 20, no. 1 (2011): 28–51.

7. Fackre, Nash, and Sanders, *What About Those Who Have Never Heard?*, 13.

8. William Smith, quoted in an interview with E. C. Briggs, *Deseret News*, January 20, 1894, cited by Donna Hill, *Joseph Smith, The First Mormon* (New York: Doubleday, 1977), 60, 460n17. See also Richard Lyman Bushman, *Joseph Smith: Rough Stone Rolling* (New York: Alfred A. Knopf, 2005), 110.

9. *The Teachings of Joseph Smith*, ed. Larry E. Dahl and Donald Q. Cannon (Salt Lake City: Bookcraft, 1997), 603.

10. *History of the Church of Jesus Christ of Latter-day Saints*, ed. B. H. Roberts, 2nd ed. rev. (Salt Lake City: Deseret Book, 1957), 4:425–26.

11. *Teachings of Joseph Smith*, 602.

For too many faithful disciples in the Church,
the message of Easter does not fall on
deaf ears but on discouraged ones.

(Doc Christensen, *Line of Authority*,
courtesy of the artist.)

"May Christ Lift Thee Up"

Brad Wilcox

For too many, the message of Easter falls on deaf ears. Elder Gerald N. Lund said, "How tragic that God so loved the world that He gave His Only Begotten Son, and the world is so blind and apathetic that it does not care. It turns away from the gift as if it were of no consequence whatever."[1] Such apathy and open rebellion breaks my heart. However, of equal concern to me is that for too many faithful disciples in the Church, the message of Easter does not fall on deaf ears but on discouraged ones. Many Saints feel defeated, as if they can never do enough and are forever falling short.

Brad Wilcox is a professor of education at Brigham Young University and a member of the Sunday School General Board. He presided over the Chile Santiago East Mission from 2003 to 2006.

The message of Easter is that Christ did not come to put us down but to lift us up.

At the end of the Book of Mormon, Moroni included a final epistle from his father in which Mormon pleads that, despite all the trials and challenges that surrounded him, Moroni would be uplifted: "May not the things which I have written grieve thee, to weigh thee down unto death; but may Christ lift thee up, and may his sufferings and death, and the showing his body unto our fathers, and his mercy and long-suffering, and the hope of his glory and of eternal life, rest in your mind forever. And may the grace of God the Father . . . and our Lord Jesus Christ . . . abide with you forever" (Moroni 9:25–26).

Mormon's message is for all of us when we are surrounded by trials, when we feel overwhelmed and beaten, when expectations seem too high and heaven seems too far out of reach. At such times Mormon's words to his son must also ring in our ears: "May Christ lift thee up."

THREE SNAPSHOTS

Consider three examples of discouraged members. Their circumstances vary, but their problems are similar.

Discouraged missionary. A zone of missionaries gathered for a conference. The elders and sisters looked forward to seeing each other and receiving instruction from their mission president. As they arrived, they exchanged news of what was going on in their various sectors. "You'll never believe it!" said one of the elders. "We found the greatest family ever!" He and his companion proceeded to tell about how they had been led to a golden family who welcomed them into their home and even came to Sunday meetings.

Another missionary piped up. "A sister in our ward asked us to teach her nephew. He is reading the Book of Mormon, and last night he accepted a baptism date."

Everyone was excited—well, almost everyone. One elder pulled at his junior companion's sleeve and stepped away from the group. "Let's go get a seat," he muttered. They entered the empty chapel where the meeting was to be held and sat down. "Why aren't we getting blessed like that?" the senior asked his companion. "Where's a golden family for us and an investigator with a baptism date? What are we doing wrong?"

The junior replied, "Elder, we're not doing anything wrong. We're obeying the rules."

"Well, we must be missing something! We are just going to have to start working harder to be worthy for the Lord's blessings."

"We *are* working hard!" said the junior. "We *are* worthy and the Lord *is* blessing us."

"But obviously that's not enough. Starting tomorrow we are going to get up earlier and go to bed later, work extra hours, and start a fast."

Busy mother. Mom gave quick hugs as she hustled her three school-aged children out the door. She was grateful it was her neighbor's turn to drive so she didn't have to be dressed yet. She turned back toward the kitchen just in time to see her preschool son reach for the orange juice and tip the carton right off the counter. She ran, but not quickly enough to catch it before it hit and sprayed juice across the kitchen floor. She yelled, "What were you thinking?" Her toddler began to cry.

What a morning! Had they read scriptures? No. She had to find her oldest son's homework. Had they had prayer? Yes, but whatever spirit that brought was now driven off by her losing her temper.

Later she berated herself in an email she wrote to a friend: "I must get up earlier so I am dressed. I need to make sure we get our scriptures in. I should keep my temper and not yell. There are just so many *must do*s and *should do*s in my life that I'm having a hard time keeping up. I know the Lord will help me if I do my part, but I can't even do that."

Perfectionist president. The Relief Society president was late for presidency meeting. It rarely happened. She was usually early, but it had been an especially trying day with six food orders to fill. The meeting opened with prayer, and the sisters turned to calendaring. As they previewed upcoming meetings, the president began to make a list of things that needed to be done in preparation. Her personality was such that she couldn't do anything halfway or delegate easily to others. The bishop called her a "200 percenter" with good reason.

Her counselor cautioned, "You are taking too much on yourself. You need to make some assignments."

She replied, "By the time I explain to one of the sisters what needs to be done and then call and remind her and then check to make sure it got done, it's just easier to simply do it myself."

"But you'll be exhausted," her counselor warned.

"I'm already exhausted," the president replied.

"Then at least do the bare minimum."

"I can't just do the bare minimum when I know I can do more," she responded. "The Lord expects my best. How can I ask for God's help if I don't give my all?"

Are the missionary, mother, and president trying to earn blessings? Are they trying to earn grace or salvation? If you asked them, they would probably say no. They are just trying to do their part—to do their best. But will their best ever be good enough? Where does such thinking stop? When things go wrong, surely they will convince themselves it is their fault for not going one more extra mile or performing one more act of service. Surely they will berate themselves for not having offered one more prayer or read one more verse of scripture. Many faithful Saints like these three rarely feel they are measuring up, and they are wearing themselves out trying.

The extreme to which this perspective can be taken became obvious in an interview I conducted with a recently returned missionary at BYU. He was anxiously engaged in many good causes, including school, work, and ward callings. He was even obediently trying to make time for dating. The list of tasks he needed to do in a day to remain even semi-guilt-free kept growing longer. I warned, "You are taking too much on yourself. You are not turning to the Lord."

He said, "Great! Now there's one more thing I have to do—turn to the Lord!"

Turning to the Lord is not one more thing to do. It is the only thing to do.[2] Christ is the vine. We are the branches. He has said, "For without me ye can do nothing" (John 15:5). In Psalm 28 we read, "The Lord is my strength and my shield; my heart trusted in him, and I am helped. . . . [I am] lift[ed] . . . up forever" (vv. 7, 9). That message sounds similar to Mormon's words, "May Christ lift thee up" (Moroni 9:25). In each of the snapshots presented and in all our lives, the solution is turning to the Lord and letting him lift us up by understanding his grace, experiencing his transforming power, and finding the hope that he alone offers.

UNDERSTAND GRACE

In many of our busy latter-day lives, what is needed is not one more sacrifice from us but rather a deeper understanding of the sacrifice of the Savior for us and the grace he offers. The LDS Bible Dictionary tells us grace is a "divine means of help or strength, given through the bounteous mercy and love of Jesus Christ" and is "made possible by his atoning sacrifice" (Bible Dictionary, "Grace," 697).

As surely as we need grace at life's finish line, we also need it to get to the finish line. Robert L. Millet wrote, "The grace of God is extended to you and me every hour of every day and is not limited to the bar of judgment."[3] Grace is the reason we can say, "[We] can do all things through Christ which strengtheneth [us]" (Philippians 4:13).

Most of us recognize our total dependence on the Lord for our salvation in the hereafter, but we may overlook our dependence on him here and now. We recognize the role of grace when Alma the Younger taught of divine forgiveness (Alma 36:18) but may overlook it when he told those in Gideon that Christ would "take upon him their infirmities, that . . . he may know according to the flesh how to succor his people" (Alma 7:12). We recognize the role of grace when Alma the Elder taught of resurrection and redemption (Mosiah 18:2) but may overlook it when he shared the answer to prayer in which the Lord said, "I will also ease the burdens which are put upon your shoulders, that even you cannot feel them upon your backs, even while you are in bondage; and this will I do that ye may stand as witnesses for me hereafter, and that ye may know of a surety that I, the Lord God, do visit my people" (Mosiah 24:14).

We read in *True to the Faith*, "In addition to needing grace for your ultimate salvation, you need this enabling power every day of your life. As you draw near to your Heavenly Father in diligence, humility, and meekness, He will uplift and strengthen you through

His grace. . . . Reliance upon His grace enables you to progress and grow in righteousness."[4]

In 2 Nephi we are reminded to rely "wholly upon the merits of him who is mighty to save" (2 Nephi 31:19). Without Christ we cannot be resurrected or forgiven. However, the ultimate goal is not just to live after we die and to be clean. Immortality and sinlessness are only two of many godlike attributes we must acquire. The ultimate goal is not just coming to Christ but becoming like him.

"The miracle of change, the miracle associated with the renovation and regeneration of fallen man, is the work of a God. . . . The transformations from a fallen nature to a spiritual nature, from worldliness to holiness, from corruption to incorruption, and from imperfection to perfection are accomplished because divine powers bring them to pass. They are acts of grace."[5]

We must not see Christ's grace as supplementing our works or our works as supplementing Christ's grace as if we need to meet some sort of minimum height requirement to enter heaven. It is not about height; it is about growth. "Too often . . . Latter-day Saints think that men and women are expected to do their 85 or 90 percent and leave the remainder, a small percentage, for Jesus to handle."[6] However, Elder M. Russell Ballard reminded us, "No matter how hard we work, no matter how much we obey, no matter how many good things we do in this life, it would not be enough were it not for Jesus Christ and His loving grace."[7]

We do not reach heaven by supplementing. We reach heaven by covenanting, and a covenant is not a cold contract between party A and party B, each doing his or her respective part. It is a warm relationship between two friends who are literally on a first-name basis, each loving and working with the other.[8] We make covenants at baptism, and hands are extended to bestow the gift of the Holy Ghost to help us. We make covenants in the temple, and a hand is extended to teach us of Christ's willingness to strengthen and help us. President Cecil O. Samuelson said, "It is that outreached hand that we call grace."[9]

Perhaps one of the reasons members of the Church avoid speaking about grace is because many Christian churches teach about the topic without a full knowledge of the plan of salvation. Robert L. Millet has said, "One of the scandals of the Christian world . . . is a seeming disregard for the simple statement of the Master: 'If ye love me, keep my commandments' (John 14:15). . . . Easy believism and cheap grace have replaced the depth of discipleship demanded by Deity."[10] Some Christians are so happy about what Christ has saved us *from* that they have not thought enough about what he has saved us *for*. They are so happy that our debt is paid that they may not have considered why the debt existed in the first place. As my friend Omar Canals puts it, many Christians see the Atonement as nothing more than a huge favor Christ did for us. Latter-day Saints see it also as a huge investment he made in us because he is transforming us.

The child's practice is not only a concrete way of showing gratitude
for Mom's loving sacrifice but also the way he is transformed.
(Cody Bell, *Boy Playing the Piano*, © Intellectual Reserve, Inc.)

BE TRANSFORMED

Christ's purpose is not just to save us but also to shape us. We
lived in a premortal world with our Father in Heaven, but we were
not like him physically or spiritually. Because we wanted to be like
him, a plan was presented that included each of us passing through
a mortal experience. God knew that an unavoidable part of that experience would be mistakes and sins, so he prepared a Savior for us.
Without mortality, our progress would have been blocked forever,
but without the Atonement the poor choices that are part of mortality would also have blocked our progress. The Atonement allows us
to be educated by mortality rather than condemned by it.[11]

Justice demands immediate perfection or punishment when we fall short. Jesus took our punishment. Jesus paid our debt to justice, and he paid that debt in full. He didn't pay it all except for a few coins. Because he paid that debt, he can now turn to us with a new arrangement. He can ask for eventual perfection and offer to strengthen, mentor, and tutor us through the developmental process, however long it takes. To that end he asks us to show faith in him, repent, make and keep covenants, seek the Holy Ghost, and endure to the end. He said, "Follow me" (Matthew 4:19) and "Keep my commandments" (John 14:15). By complying, we are not paying the demands of justice—not even the smallest part. Instead, we are showing appreciation for what Jesus Christ did by using the Atonement to improve ourselves and live a life like his.

Over the last few years, I have shared the following analogy, which has proven helpful for some: Christ's arrangement with us is similar to a mom providing music lessons for her child. Mom, who pays the piano teacher, can require her child to practice. By so doing, she is not attempting to recover the cost of the lessons, but to help the child take full advantage of this opportunity to live on a higher level. Her joy is found not in getting her investment back but in seeing it used. The child's practice is not only a concrete way of showing gratitude for Mom's loving sacrifice but also the way he is transformed.

If the child, in his immaturity, sees Mom's expectation to practice as unnecessary or overly burdensome, it is because he doesn't yet share her perspective. When Christ's expectations feel trying to us, perhaps it is because we do not yet see through his eyes. We do not yet understand what he is trying to make of us. A God who requires nothing of us is making nothing of us, and our Heavenly Father does not work this way.

Elder Dallin H. Oaks has said, "The repenting sinner must suffer for his sins, but this suffering has a different purpose than punishment or payment. Its purpose is *change*."[12] Let's put that in terms of the music lessons: the child must practice the piano, but this practice has a different purpose than punishment or payment. Its purpose is change.

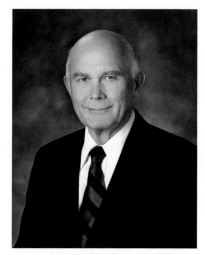

Elder Dallin H. Oaks
(© Intellectual Reserve, Inc.)

Occasionally I have seen a man walking near BYU campus carrying a large cross bearing the words "Saved by Grace." He seems to think Latter-day Saints are missing that message. On the contrary, we acknowledge and agree that we are saved by grace, but we also recognize that salvation is only part of the message of Christ's cross. Christ came to save us by bridging the abyss between humans and the divine, but then what? Is the whole goal to make peace with God and be close to him? No.

Latter-day Saints know there is much more ahead. We believe in life after death, but we also believe in life after salvation. Christ came to save us and to transform us. This knowledge can offer us great hope.

FIND HOPE

Hope brings perspective when we consider the past and new motivation as we look toward the future. One young man, Reed Rasband, wrote the following in my mission preparation class: "I knew the Atonement brought comfort and forgiveness because I had experienced those blessings, but I failed to see how the blessings of the Atonement were continually pouring over me. In the past I used the Atonement only when my life got hard or when I made a mistake. My use of the Atonement was limited because I did not realize Christ's power to help me was constantly there—even when I did not think I needed help. One of the pieces of the puzzle I was missing was grace. Grace to me was a vague, diffuse source of divine help that I had difficulty channeling."

Reed went on to explain that he had previously believed that grace—divine assistance and enabling power—must be earned by works, even if the works were minimal. He wrote: "This paradigm was easy to understand. Jesus had his part and so did I. I worked hard to fulfill my share, trying to live as righteously as I could to be worthy of His grace. I knew I only had to do my small part, but deep inside I wondered how I would ever know when my part was completed. I realize now the problem with this outlook was not striving for improvement; it was that I did not fully recognize Jesus as being the improver."

Without this understanding, Reed became frustrated because he felt that any steps toward self-betterment were all his responsibility. Even if he improved one aspect of his life, he would still see many others where he was not up to par. Then he would work really hard at one of those and find that he had slipped backward on the first. Reed knew he could lay his burdens at Jesus' feet, but he was determined to have them all clean, wrapped up nicely, and even tied with a bow so they would be acceptable.

A turning point came for Reed when he considered Christ's perfect attributes. Reed wrote: "Only as I began to understand Christ's perfect love could I begin to understand His grace and Atonement. Jesus does not just love me when I am sinning or hurting. He loves me all the time and is willing to help me all the time. He wants me to become like Him." Reed realized divine help was not just available when he was at the end of his rope—it *was* his rope. Reed didn't need to earn Christ's help. He didn't need to deserve it. Reed insightfully wrote, "Grace is no more earned than Christ's love is deserved."

Reed felt hope when he realized that works are important not because they are a requirement for receiving grace but because they develop from it. They are how we channel, use, and show appreciation for the priceless gift. Grace is not the absence of God's high expectations but the presence of God's power.

Like Reed, I have felt great hope as I realize that in this school of mortality we are not alone. We have divine help with our homework. One of my favorite names for Jesus is *Emmanuel.* We are told its meaning in scripture: "God with us" (Matthew 1:23). Is there a better definition of grace than this? Much is required of us in this perfecting process, but God and Christ are *with us* throughout the entire transforming journey.

FEEL UPLIFTED

The message of Easter is Christ's Atonement. Because of it, we can live again after we die, and we can be forgiven of our sins. But the message of Easter does not stop there. Because of the Atonement, we can be consoled in our sorrows and afflictions. But the message of Easter doesn't stop there either. Because of the Atonement, we can ultimately become like Jesus. This idea gives great meaning to Mormon's words, "May Christ lift thee up" (Moroni 9:25). The word *lift* means to elevate or raise to a higher mood or position, but it also means to raise in rank or condition. Christ lifts our condtion as we turn to him by understanding his grace, experiencing his transformation, and finding the hope that he alone can give.

To the discouraged missionary we say, "Take heart! Christ will lift you up." Blessings are not just awaiting extra-milers. Blessings are enabling each mile and extra mile. Grace is not a prize for the worthy but power to become worthy. To the busy mom we say, "Don't quit! Christ will lift you up." Let's not get so focused on checking items off our to-do list that we forget why God gave us the list in the first place. We are not called human doings. We are called human beings. God knows that becoming takes time and that some days are better than others. To the "200 percenter" Relief Society president we say, "Thanks for your sincere efforts! But remember you are working not just *for* God but *with* him. Christ will lift you up." God uses people to finish his work, but he also uses his work to finish people. Because he knows we can't give our all—not all the time—he is willing to accept any sincere effort. We don't have to be perfect right now. We just have to be willing to be perfected.

Christ did not come to put us down but to lift us up. This is the message of Easter that is needed by a deaf world and also by discouraged Saints. When we feel we can't do enough, we can remember he did more than enough (Ether 12:26; Moroni 10:32). When we become painfully aware of our weakness, we can marvel at his strength (see Psalm 136:12). When we feel we have fallen from grace, we can realize it is actually grace that lifts us up. Mormon's words to Moroni are also written to us: "May Christ lift thee up. . . . And may the grace of God the Father . . . and our Lord Jesus Christ . . . abide with you forever" (Moroni 9:25–26).

NOTES

1. Gerald N. Lund, "What the Atoning Sacrifice Meant for Jesus," in *My Redeemer Lives*, ed. Richard Neitzel Holzapfel and Kent P. Jackson (Provo, UT: Religious Studies Center, Brigham Young University; Salt Lake City: Deseret Book, 2011), 46.

2. See Stephen E. Robinson, *Believing Christ* (Salt Lake City: Deseret Book, 1992), 65–69.

3. Robert L. Millet, "What We Worship," in *My Redeemer Lives*, 85.

4. *True to the Faith: A Gospel Reference* (Salt Lake City: The Church of Jesus Christ of Latter-day Saints, 2004), 78.

5. Robert L. Millet, *By Grace We Are Saved* (Salt Lake City: Bookcraft, 1989), 19, 86.

6. Millet, "What We Worship," 84.

7. M. Russell Ballard, "Building Bridges of Understanding," *Ensign*, June 1998, 65.

8. Truman G. Madsen, *The Temple: Where Heaven Meets Earth* (Salt Lake City: Deseret Book, 2008), 69.

9. Cecil O. Samuelson, "'Be Ye Therefore Perfect'" (devotional address, September 6, 2011, Brigham Young University, Provo, UT).

10. Millet, "What We Worship," 86–87.

11. See Bruce C. Hafen and Marie K. Hafen, *The Belonging Heart* (Salt Lake City: Deseret Book, 1994), 77.

12. Dallin H. Oaks, *The Lord's Way* (Salt Lake City: Deseret Book, 1991), 223; emphasis in original.

INDEX